Sex, Race, and
the Sovereignty of God

T0340631

OTHER BOOKS BY JOHN PIPER

Desiring God

Don't Waste Your Life

Future Grace

God Is the Gospel

A Godward Life

A Hunger for God

Let the Nations Be Glad!

The Pleasures of God

Providence

Reading the Bible Supernaturally

The Satisfied Soul

Seeing and Savoring Jesus Christ

27 Servants of Sovereign Joy

Taste and See

When I Don't Desire God

SEX, RACE,

and the

SOVEREIGNTY

of

GOD

SWEET *and* BITTER PROVIDENCE

in the BOOK OF RUTH

JOHN PIPER

WHEATON, ILLINOIS

Sex, Race, and the Sovereignty of God
Formerly published as *A Sweet and Bitter Providence*

Copyright © 2010, 2022 by Desiring God Foundation

Published by Crossway
        1300 Crescent Street
        Wheaton, Illinois 60187

Cover design: Jordan Singer

First printing 2010

Reprinted with new title 2022

Printed in the United States of America

Unless otherwise indicated, Scripture quotations are taken from the ESV® Bible (The Holy Bible: English Standard Version®), copyright © 2001 by Crossway, a publishing ministry of Good News Publishers. Used by permission. All rights reserved. The ESV text may not be quoted in any publication made available to the public by a Creative Commons license. The ESV may not be translated into any other language.

Scripture quotations marked KJV are from the King James Version of the Bible. Public domain.

Scripture quotations marked NASB are taken from the New American Standard Bible®, copyright © 1960, 1971, 1977, 1995 by The Lockman Foundation. Used by permission. All rights reserved. www.lockman.org.

Scripture quotations marked NIV are taken from the Holy Bible: New International Version®. NIV®. Copyright © 1973, 1978, 1984 by International Bible Society. Used by permission of Zondervan. All rights reserved worldwide.

Trade paperback ISBN: 978-1-4335-8178-6

PDF ISBN: 978-1-4335-8179-3

Mobipocket ISBN: 978-1-4335-8180-9

ePub ISBN: 978-1-4335-8181-6

Library of Congress Cataloging-in-Publication Data

Piper, John, 1946–
  A sweet and bitter providence : sex, race, and the
  sovereignty of God / John Piper.
    p. cm.
  Includes bibliographical references and index.
  ISBN 978-1-4335-1437-1 (hc)
  1. Bible O.T. Ruth—Commentaries. I. Title.
BS1315.53.P67   2010
222'.3506—dc22   2009021018

Crossway is a publishing ministry of Good News Publishers.

VP		31	30	29	28	27	26	25	24	23	22
15	14	13	12	11	10	9	8	7	6	5	4	3	2	1

To
Noël and Talitha
women of worth

"Do not call me Naomi; call me Mara, for
the Almighty has dealt very bitterly with me.
I went away full, and the LORD has brought me
back empty. Why call me Naomi, when the LORD
has testified against me and the Almighty
has brought calamity upon me?"
. . . Naomi said to her daughter-in-law, "May he be
blessed by the LORD, whose kindness has not
forsaken the living or the dead!"

RUTH 1:20–21; 2:20

CONTENTS

INTRODUCTION

RUTH IS A VERY OLD BOOK. The events took place over three thousand years ago. Could it be relevant and helpful for your life? I think so. The sovereignty of God, the sexual nature of man, and the gospel never change. And since God is still sovereign, and you are male or female, and Christ is alive and powerful, the book has a message for you.

I don't know you or your circumstances well enough to say for sure that you should read this book. You must decide. To be sure, there are other things to do that are just as important—like telling your neighbor about Jesus. So let me simply tell you why I think you might be helped if you join me in listening to the message of Ruth. I'll make these seven reasons brief, so you can decide and be on your way or stay.

The Word of God

First, the book of Ruth is part of the Scriptures, which Jesus loved. He said, "Scripture cannot be broken" (John 10:35). He said, "Until heaven and earth pass away, not an iota, not a dot, will pass from the Law [a reference to the Scriptures] until all is accomplished" (Matthew 5:18). And best of all he said, "The Scriptures . . . bear witness about me" (John 5:39).

The reason these Scriptures—including Ruth—cannot be broken is that they are God's word. "All Scripture is breathed out by God" (2 Tim. 3:16). "Men spoke from God as they were carried along by the Holy Spirit" (2 Pet. 1:21). Therefore, the message of Ruth is unwaveringly true. It's a rock to stand on when the terrain of ideas feels like quicksand. It's an anchor to hold us when tides are ripping.

But the best thing about the Scriptures is that they give hope, because they point to Jesus Christ. They were "written for our instruction, that through endurance and through the encouragement of the Scriptures we might have hope" (Rom. 15:4). The message of Ruth is filled with God-inspired hope.

A Love Story

Second, Ruth is a love story. One commentary suggests that it may be "the most beautiful short story ever written."[1] There are some heart-stopping moments. Not often do we get the richest and deepest truth in the form of a passionate love story. The way Ruth and Boaz find each

---

[1] F. B. Huey, *Ruth, The Expositor's Bible Commentary*, Vol. 3, ed. Frank E. Gaebelein (Grand Rapids, MI: Zondervan, 1992), 509.

other is the stuff of epics. It involves God's sovereign rule over nations and reaches across thousands of years in its purpose. But the story is the flesh-and-blood experience of one family living the unexpected plan of God.

Manhood and Womanhood

Third, the book of Ruth is the portrait of beautiful, noble manhood and womanhood. The greatness of manhood and womanhood is more than sex. It is more than a throbbing love story. In a day when movies and television and advertising and the Internet portray masculinity and femininity in the lowest ways, we are in great need of stories that elevate the magnificent meaning of manhood and womanhood.

In making sex the main thing, and in flattering or reversing the differences between men and women, the modern world is losing the glory and beauty and depth and power of what sexuality becomes when it runs like a deep and mighty river between the high banks of righteousness. Ruth and Boaz are extraordinary. Men and women today need heroes like this.

Ethnocentrism

Fourth, the story of Ruth addresses one of the great issues of our time: racial and ethnic diversity and harmony.

Racism and all manner of ethnocentrisms are as common today around the world as they ever have been. The shrinking of the planet into immediate access on the Internet has brought thousands of strange people and strange patterns of life into our lives—and put our strangeness into their lives. Diversity is a given in this world. The question is how we will think and feel and act about it.

Consider a few facts from the U. S. Census Bureau about what is in store for America:

> Between 2010 and 2020 the percentage of those Americans who reported their race as white only (no mixture) fell by 8.6%. In that same period, the "multiracial population" increased from 9 million to 33.8 million, a 276% increase. The Hispanic or Latino population increased by 23% in that same decade. One summary describes the future like this: "The new statistics project that the nation will become 'minority white' in 2045. During that year, whites will comprise 49.7 percent of the population in contrast to 24.6 percent for Hispanics, 13.1 percent for blacks, 7.9 percent for Asians, and 3.8 percent for multiracial populations."[2]

[2] "Improved Race and Ethnicity Measures Reveal U.S. Population Is Much More Multiracial," United States Census Bureau website, accessed March 23, 2022, https://www.census.gov; and "The US Will Become 'Minority White' in 2045, Census Projects," Brookings website, accessed March 23, 2022, https://www.brookings.edu.

Ruth is an "unclean" pagan Moabitess. But she is drawn into faith and into the lineage of Jesus Christ, the Son of God. Her marriage is an interracial marriage. There are lessons here that we need as much today as ever.

The Sovereignty of God

Fifth, the most prominent purpose of the book of Ruth is to bring the calamities and sorrows of life under the sway of God's providence and show us that God's purposes are good. It is not a false statement when Naomi, Ruth's mother-in-law, says, "The Almighty has dealt very bitterly with me. I went away full, and the LORD has brought me back empty. . . . The Almighty has brought calamity upon me" (Ruth 1:20–21).

That is true. But here's the question the book answers: *Is God's bitter providence the last word?* Are bitter ingredients (like vanilla extract) put in the mixer to make the cake taste bad? Everywhere I look in the world today, whether near or far, the issue for real people in real life is, *Can I trust and love the God who has dealt me this painful hand in life?* That is the question the book of Ruth intends to answer.[3]

[3] To see how the whole Bible answers this question, see John Piper, *Providence* (Wheaton, IL: Crossway, 2021).

Risk-Taking Love

Sixth, the gift of hope in God's providence is meant to overflow in radical acts of love for hurting people. The book of Ruth is not in the Bible merely to help us think right thoughts about God. Nor merely to give us hope in his good providence. That hope-filled confidence is meant to release radical, risk-taking love. It's there to make you a new kind of person—a person who is able "to do justice, and to love kindness, and to walk humbly with your God" (Mic. 6:8).

The Glory of Christ

Seventh, the book of Ruth aims to show that all of history, even its darkest hours, serves to magnify the glory of God's grace. In surprising ways, a thousand years before Christ, this book glorifies his saving work on the cross, as we will see. Ruth is about the work of God in the darkest of times to prepare the world for the glories of Jesus Christ.

I invite you to join me as we walk together through this amazing story.

CHAPTER ONE

SWEET AND BITTER PROVIDENCE

Where you go I will go, and where you lodge
I will lodge. Your people shall be my people,
and your God my God. Where you die I will die,
and there will I be buried.
May the LORD do so to me and more also
if anything but death parts me from you.

RUTH 1:16–17

In the days when the judges ruled there was a famine in the land, and a man of Bethlehem in Judah went to sojourn in the country of Moab, he and his wife and his two sons. ² The name of the man was Elimelech and the name of his wife Naomi, and the names of his two sons were Mahlon and Chilion. They were Ephrathites from Bethlehem in Judah. They went into the country of Moab and remained there. ³ But Elimelech, the husband of Naomi, died, and she was left with her two sons. ⁴ These took Moabite wives; the name of the one was Orpah and the name of the other Ruth. They lived there about ten years, ⁵ and both Mahlon and Chilion died, so that the woman was left without her two sons and her husband.

⁶ Then she arose with her daughters-in-law to return from the country of Moab, for she had heard in the fields of Moab that the LORD had visited his people and given them food. ⁷ So she set out from the place where she was with her two daughters-in-law, and they went on the way to return to the land of Judah. ⁸ But Naomi said to her two daughters-in-law, "Go, return each of you to her mother's house. May the LORD deal kindly with you, as you have dealt with the dead and with me. ⁹ The LORD grant that you may find rest, each of you in the house of her husband!" Then she kissed them, and they lifted up their voices and wept. ¹⁰ *And they said to her, "No, we will return with you to your people." * ¹¹ *But Naomi said, "Turn back, my daughters; why will you go with me? Have I yet sons in my womb that they may become your husbands?* ¹² *Turn back, my daughters; go your way, for I am too old to have a husband. If I should say I have hope, even if I should have a husband this night and should bear sons,* ¹³ *would you therefore wait till they were grown? Would you therefore refrain from marrying? No, my daughters, for it is exceedingly bitter to me for your sake that the hand of the LORD has gone out against me." * ¹⁴ *Then they lifted up their voices and wept again. And Orpah kissed her mother-in-law, but Ruth clung to her.*

¹⁵ *And she said, "See, your sister-in-law has gone back to her people and to her gods; return after your sister-in-law." * ¹⁶ *But Ruth said, "Do not urge me to leave you or to return from following you. For where you go I will go, and where you lodge I will lodge. Your people shall be my people, and your God my God.* ¹⁷ *Where you die I will die, and there will I be buried. May the LORD do so to me and more also if anything but death parts me from you."*

18 And when Naomi saw that she was determined to go with her, she said no more.

19 So the two of them went on until they came to Bethlehem. And when they came to Bethlehem, the whole town was stirred because of them. And the women said, "Is this Naomi?" 20 She said to them, "Do not call me Naomi; call me Mara, for the Almighty has dealt very bitterly with me. 21 I went away full, and the LORD has brought me back empty. Why call me Naomi, when the LORD has testified against me and the Almighty has brought calamity upon me?"

22 So Naomi returned, and Ruth the Moabite her daughter-in-law with her, who returned from the country of Moab. And they came to Bethlehem at the beginning of barley harvest. (Ruth 1)

The Prostitute and the Moabite

According to the first verse of the book of Ruth, the story took place during the time of the judges. That's why Ruth comes right after the book called *Judges* in our Bibles. The time of the judges was a four-hundred-year period after Israel entered the Promised Land under the leadership of Joshua and before there were any kings in Israel (roughly 1400 B.C. to 1000 B.C.).

Although some generations may be left out of the genealogy in Ruth 4:18–22, Boaz, who marries Ruth, is linked as a descendant from Rahab, the converted prostitute who lived when Israel first came into the Promised Land (Josh. 2:1, 3; 6:17, 23). We learn this from the genealogy of Jesus in Matthew 1:5. This signals to us that remarkable things are in the offing. Why would a prostitute and a Moabitess be mentioned back-to-back in the genealogy of Jesus? Why would they be mentioned at all? We are getting in at the ground level of something amazing.

God at Work in the Worst of Times

You can see from the last verse of the book of Judges what sort of period it was. Judges 21:25 says, "In those days there was no king in Israel. Everyone did what was right in his own eyes." It was a very dark time in Israel. The same gloomy pattern happened again and again: the people would sin, God would send enemies against them, the people would cry for help, and God would mercifully raise up a judge to deliver them (Judg. 2:16–19).

From all outward appearances, God's purposes for

righteousness and glory in Israel were failing. But what
the book of Ruth does for us is give us a glimpse into the
hidden work of God during the worst of times.

Consider the last verse of Ruth (4:22). The child
born to Ruth and Boaz during the period of the judges
is Obed. Obed becomes the father of Jesse, and Jesse
becomes the father of David who led Israel to her greatest heights of glory. One of the main messages of this
little book is that God is at work in the worst of times.

Putting in Place the Ancestry of Christ

Even through the sins of his people, God plots for their
glory. It was true at the national level. And we will see
that it is true at the personal, family level too. God is
at work in the worst of times. He is at work doing a
thousand things no one can see but him. In the case of
this story, God is at work preparing the way for Christ
in a manner no one can see.[1] The reason we know it is
because the book ends by connecting Ruth and Boaz
with David the king. The last words of the book are
"Boaz fathered Obed, Obed fathered Jesse, and Jesse
fathered David" (4:21–22).

---

[1]For a more extended treatment on how God throughout the Bible plots the
good of his people even through their sins, see John Piper, *Spectacular Sins:
And Their Global Purpose for the Glory of Christ* (Wheaton, IL: Crossway,
2008).

Jesus identified himself as "the son of David" (Matt. 22:41–46). He forged a link straight from himself, over all the intervening generations, to David and Jesse and Obed and Ruth. Knowing how this book ends gives us a sense, as we begin, that nothing will be insignificant here. Huge things are at stake. God is putting in place the ancestry of Jesus the Messiah, whose kingdom will endure forever (Isa. 9:7).

Behind a Frowning Providence

As a means to that end—and everything is a means to glorifying Christ—the book of Ruth reveals the hidden hand of God in the bitter experiences of his people. The point of this book is not just that God is preparing the way for the coming of the King of Glory, but that he is doing it in such a way that all of us should learn that the worst of times are not wasted. They are not wasted globally, historically, or personally.

When you think he is farthest from you, or has even turned against you, the truth is that as you cling to him, he is laying foundation stones of greater happiness in your life.

> *Judge not the Lord by feeble sense,*
> *But trust him for his grace;*

Behind a frowning providence
He hides a smiling face.[2]

What William Cowper says in these lines is a description of how God brings about the eternal salvation of his people. It's the way he governs history, and it is the way he governs our lives. The book of Ruth is one of the most graphic stories of how God hides his smiling face behind a frowning providence.

The Miseries of Naomi

Verses 1–5 describe the misery of Naomi—the frowning providence, as we will see. Naomi is one of the three main characters in this drama. She will become the mother-in-law of Ruth. She is an Israelite with her husband Elimelech and two sons Mahlon and Chilion. They are from Bethlehem where we know Jesus will be born one day—which raises our awareness again of how explosive this book is with connections to the Messiah.

Naomi, not her husband or sons or Ruth, is the focus of the first chapter of Ruth. This chapter is about her miseries—her bitter providence. The first misery (1:1) is a famine in Judah where Naomi and her husband Elimelech and her sons live. Naomi knows who causes

[2]William Cowper, "God Moves in a Mysterious Way" (1774).

famines. God does. Perhaps she learned this from the Scriptures, which say in Leviticus 26:3–4, "If you walk in my statutes and observe my commandments and do them, then I will give you your rains in their season, and the land shall yield its increase." In other words, God rules the rain. When the rains are withheld, this is the hard hand of God.

Is This Blasphemous or Comforting?

Please know that I am aware of how unacceptable this truth is to some. That horrific suffering serves God's purposes is not seen as good news by many. Flesh-and-blood calamities, like the tsunami of December 2004, are so devastating in the human agony they cause that many Christians cannot ascribe them to the plan of God. For example, David Hart wrote in the *Wall Street Journal*,

> When confronted by the sheer savage immensity of worldly suffering—when we see the entire littoral rim of the Indian Ocean strewn with tens of thousands of corpses, a third of them children's—no Christian is licensed to utter odious banalities about God's inscrutable counsels or blasphemous suggestions that all this mysteriously serves God's good ends.[3]

[3]David B. Hart, "Tremors of Doubt," *Wall Street Journal*, December 31, 2004, accessed 12-3-08, http://opinionjournal.com.

These are strong words. And I strongly disagree with them. It is the message of the book of Ruth, as we will see, that all things mysteriously serve God's good ends. Thousands of Christians who have walked through fire and have seen horrors embrace God's control of all things as the comfort and hope of their lives. It is not comforting or hopeful in their pain to tell them that God is not in control. Giving Satan the decisive control or ascribing pain to chance is not true or helpful. When the world is crashing in, we need assurance that God reigns over it all.

I write these things because they are true. I also write them because after thirty-five years of ministering to real people, I know they are precious to those who suffer. The people who most cherish the sovereignty of God in suffering are those exposed to the greatest dangers.

A Sovereign Bullet

For example, on April 20, 2001, the Peruvian Air Force shot down a missionary plane, mistaking it for a drug courier. In the plane were the pilot Kevin Donaldson and a missionary family, Jim and Veronica Bowers and their two children, seven-month-old Charity and six-year-old Cory. Veronica had Charity in her lap sitting in the back of the Cessna 185. As the bullets sprayed the plane, one of them entered Veronica's back and passed through her and into her daughter. Both died. The pilot, with shattered knees, crash-landed the plane in a river, and the other three survived.

Seven days later at the memorial service in Fruitport, Michigan, Jim Bowers gave his testimony and explained why the sovereignty of God in the deaths of his wife and daughter was the rock under his feet.

> Most of all I want to thank God. He's a sovereign God. I'm finding that out more now. . . . Some of you might ask, "Why thank God?" . . . Could this really be God's plan for Roni and Charity; God's plan for Cory and me and our family? I'd like to tell you why I believe so.[4]

He goes on to give fifteen reasons. In that context, he says, "Roni and Charity were instantly killed by the same bullet. (Would you say that's a stray bullet?) And it didn't reach Kevin, who was right in front of Charity; it stayed in Charity. That was a sovereign bullet."

But what about the Peruvian fighter pilots? Didn't they have wills? Didn't they make mistakes or, per-

[4]Quoted from an online transcript of Jim Bowers's message. Accessed 5-1-09; www.rockvalleybiblechurch.org.

haps, even sin against an innocent missionary family? Jim Bowers said, "Those people who did that simply were used by God. Whether you want to believe it or not. I believe it. They were used by Him, by God, to accomplish His purpose in this, maybe similar to the Roman soldiers whom God used to put Christ on the cross."[5]

We will see from the story of Ruth and from the cross of Christ that in this life our hope in the next depends on God's reign over all things. It may be hard to embrace when the pain is great, but far worse would be the weakness of God and his inability to stop the blowing of the wind and the flight of a bullet.

The Parallels with Joseph and Egypt

Naomi knew that God ruled the rain and, therefore, the famine. This was implicit in the Scriptures. Or she may have learned it from the story of Joseph. In fact, there are some striking parallels between Naomi's circumstances and Joseph's. Joseph, the son of Jacob, was sold into slavery in Egypt by his own brothers (Genesis 37:28). In the end, this would prove to be the salvation of the very brothers who sold him. Indeed, it would save

[5]Ibid.

the entire people of Israel—and preserve the ancestral line of the Messiah. A famine struck the land of Israel, and Joseph proved to be the one who provided food for his family.

The parallels in Naomi's situation are that she was taken to a foreign land and that a famine threatened her life and the life of God's people and the ancestral line of the Messiah was preserved in a way no one would have dreamed—a Moabite woman became the ancestor of the Son of God.

The point I am focusing on here is that Naomi knew that famines were from God. Psalm 105:16–17 describes God's action in connection with Joseph's sale into Egypt and the famine that came. It says that God "summoned" the famine and that God had "sent" Joseph. In other words, the famine and the rescue from famine were planned by God. The psalm says, "When [God] summoned a famine on the land and broke all supply of bread, he had sent a man ahead of them, Joseph, who was sold as a slave."

This is what Naomi believed about the famine of her own day. It was of God. This is going to be very important in deciding whether she is right when she says later in this chapter, "The Almighty has brought calamity upon me" (Ruth 1:21).

Playing with Fire

After we learn that there is a famine in Israel, we see the family leaving Israel and going to Moab to escape the famine. Moab is a pagan land with foreign gods (Ruth 1:15; Judg. 10:6). Going to Moab was playing with fire. God had called his people to be separate from the surrounding lands. So when Naomi's husband dies (Ruth 1:3), what could she feel but that the judgment of God had followed her and added grief to famine? "The hand of the LORD has gone out against me" (1:13).

Then her two sons take Moabite wives, one named Orpah, the other named Ruth (1:4). And again the hand of God falls. Verse 5 sums up Naomi's tragedy after ten years of childless marriages: "Both Mahlon and Chilion died, so that the woman was left without her two sons and her husband." A famine, a move to pagan Moab, the death of her husband, the marriage of her sons to foreign wives, ten years of apparent childlessness for both of her daughters-in-law, and the death of her sons—blow after blow, tragedy upon tragedy. Now what?

"The Hand of the LORD Has Gone Out against Me"

In verse 6, Naomi gets word that "the LORD had visited his people and given them food." So she decides to return to Judah. Her two daughters-in-law, Ruth and Orpah, go with her, partway it seems, but then in verses 8–13 she tries to persuade them to go back home. I think there are three reasons why the writer devotes so much space to Naomi's effort to turn Ruth and Orpah back.

First, the scene emphasizes Naomi's misery. For example, verse 11: "But Naomi said, 'Turn back, my daughters; why will you go with me? Have I yet sons in my womb that they may become your husbands?'" In other words, Naomi has nothing to offer them. Her condition is worse than theirs. If they try to be faithful to her and to the name of their husbands, they will find nothing but pain. So she concludes at the end of verse 13, "No, my daughters, for it is exceedingly bitter to me for your sake that the hand of the LORD has gone out against me." In other words, *Don't come with me because God is against me. Your life may become as bitter as mine.*

The Strange Custom of Marrying Kinsmen

The second reason for verses 8–13 is to prepare us for a custom in Israel that is going to turn everything around for Naomi in the following chapters. The custom was that when an Israelite husband died, his brother or near relative was to marry the widow and preserve the brother's name (Deut. 25:5–10). Naomi is referring to this custom (in Ruth 1:11) when she says she has no sons to marry Ruth and Orpah. She thinks it is hopeless for Ruth and Orpah to remain committed to the family name. She doesn't remember, evidently, that there is another relative named Boaz who might perform the duty of a brother.

There's a lesson here. When we have decided that God is against us, we usually exaggerate our hopelessness. We become so bitter we can't see the rays of light peeping out around the clouds. It was God who broke the famine and opened the way home (1:6). It was God who preserved a kinsman to continue Naomi's line (2:20). And it was God who constrains Ruth to stay with Naomi. But Naomi is so embittered by God's hard providence that she doesn't see his mercy at work in her life.

"Your God Will Be My God"

The third reason for verses 8–13 is to make Ruth's faithfulness to Naomi appear amazing. Verse 14 says that Orpah kissed Naomi goodbye, but Ruth clung to her. Not even another entreaty in verse 15 can get Ruth to leave: "See, your sister-in-law has gone back to her people and to her gods; return after your sister-in-law." No. She will stay. This is all the more amazing after Naomi's grim description of their future with her. Ruth is still young (2:5; 4:12). Nevertheless, she stays with Naomi in spite of an apparent future of widowhood and childlessness. Naomi painted the future very dark, and Ruth took her hand and walked into it with her.

The amazing words of Ruth are found in 1:16–17,

> Do not urge me to leave you or to return from following you. For where you go I will go, and where you lodge I will lodge. Your people shall be my people, and your God my God. Where you die I will die, and there will I be buried. May the Lord do so to me and more also if anything but death parts me from you.

The more you ponder these words, the more amazing they become. Ruth's commitment to her destitute mother-in-law is simply astonishing.

First, it means leaving her own family and land. Second, it means, as far as she knows, a life of widowhood and childlessness, because Naomi has no man to give her, and if she married a non-relative, Ruth's commitment to Naomi's family would be lost. Third, it means going to an unknown land with a new people and new customs and new language. Fourth, it was a commitment even more radical than marriage: "Where you die I will die, and there will I be buried" (1:17). In other words, she will never return home, not even if Naomi dies.

But the most amazing commitment of all is this: "Your God [will be] my God" (1:16). Naomi has just said in verse 13, "The hand of the LORD has gone out against me." Naomi's experience of God was bitterness. But in spite of this, Ruth forsakes her religious heritage and makes the God of Israel her God. Perhaps she had made that commitment years before, when her husband told her of the great love of God for Israel and his power at the Red Sea and his glorious purpose of peace and righteousness. Somehow or other, Ruth had come to trust in Naomi's God in spite of Naomi's bitter experiences.

"She Laughs at the Time to Come"

Here we have a picture of God's ideal woman—and we will see more of her quality later. Faith in God that sees beyond present bitter setbacks. Freedom from the securities and comforts of the world. Courage to venture into the unknown and the strange. Radical commitment in the relationships appointed by God. This is the woman of Proverbs 31:25 who looks into the future with confidence in God and laughs at the coming troubles: "Strength and dignity are her clothing, and she laughs at the time to come." Ruth is one of "the holy women who hoped in God . . . [and did] not fear anything that is frightening" (1 Pet. 3:5–6).

It is a beautiful thing to watch a woman like this serve Christ with courage. I have been able to do it up close, especially in recent years, since my wife Noël is freer to travel than when she was raising four boys. Now, with only our teenage daughter Talitha at home, Noël will travel around the world for the cause of missions and for the care of people with disabilities. If she can, she simply takes Talitha along. If not, Talitha and I make do at home.

Noël seems fearless to me in the way she ventures into difficult places. When we moved into Phillips Neighborhood in south Minneapolis—the kind of neighborhood where you don't homestead a house for investment purposes—she never batted an eye. This is where we have lived for almost thirty years. Urban stories could be told, but there would be none about my wife's fear. She is Ruth-like. And with a prayer and dream, "Ruth" is Talitha's middle name. O that all our churches might breed Ruth-like women!

"Call Me *Mara*"

So Ruth and Naomi return together to Bethlehem in Judah. "And when they came to Bethlehem, the whole town was stirred because of them. And the women said, 'Is this Naomi?'" (Ruth 1:19). That is a painful question not only because they see that she is older and with no husband and no sons, but also because the name *Naomi* means "pleasant" or "sweet." So she responds,

> Do not call me Naomi; call me Mara, for the Almighty has dealt very bitterly with me. I went away full, and the LORD has brought me back empty. Why call me Naomi, when the LORD has testified against me and the Almighty has brought calamity upon me? (Ruth 1:20–21)

What do you make of Naomi's theology?

At Least She Makes No Excuses for God

I would take Naomi's theology any day over the sentimental views of God that permeate so many churches today. Endless excuses are made for God's sovereignty.

Naomi is unshaken and sure about three things: God exists, God is sovereign, and God has afflicted her.

The problem with Naomi is that the story of Joseph has not gotten into her bones. We mentioned that story earlier. Joseph too went into a foreign country. He was sold as a slave. He was framed by an adulteress and put in prison. He had every reason to say, with Naomi, "The Almighty has dealt bitterly with me." But he was never embittered against God. God turned it all for Joseph's personal good and for Israel's national good.

The key lesson in Genesis 50:20 is this: "As for you [Joseph says to his brothers], you meant evil against me, but God meant it for good." Naomi is right to believe in a sovereign, almighty God who governs the affairs of nations and families—and gives each day its part of pain and pleasure, as the old Swedish hymn says.[6] But she needs to open her eyes—the eyes of her heart—to the signs of his merciful purposes.

---

[6]Karolina W. Sandell-Berg, "Day by Day" (1865):
Day by day, and with each passing moment,
Strength I find, to meet my trials here;
Trusting in my Father's wise bestowment,
I've no cause for worry or for fear.

He whose heart is kind beyond all measure,
Gives unto each day what He deems best—
Lovingly, its part of pain and pleasure,
Mingling toil with peace and rest.

Embittered Eyes Become Blind

It was God who took away the famine and opened a way home. Naomi "had heard in the fields of Moab that the LORD had visited his people and given them food" (Ruth 1:6). Just as surely as God brought the famine, God took it away. Naomi could see that. But she could not see all that God was doing. Later she will be able to look back, in the same way we can when we read the book a second time, and see the pointers of hope.

For example, notice the delicate touch of hope at the end of 1:22: "And they came to Bethlehem at the beginning of barley harvest." If Naomi could only see what this is going to mean. The barley field is where Ruth will meet Boaz, her future husband.

Not only that, Naomi needs to open her eyes to Ruth. What a gift! What a blessing! Yet as she and Ruth stand before the people of Bethlehem, Naomi says in verse 21, "The LORD has brought me back empty." Not so, Naomi! You are so weary with the night of adversity that you can't see the dawn of rejoicing.

It may help at his point to give a personal testimony from John Knight. John is a senior director at Desiring God.[7] He has known what it is like to be treated as

7See www.desiringGod.org.

Naomi was and to respond the way Naomi did. He also gives us a glimpse of how God mercifully and patiently leads his people out of the blindness of bitterness. The following was a birthday letter[8] to his son Paul who is blind and autistic.

> The 4th of July is a different sort of "Independence Day" for me. On July 4, 1995, my multiply disabled son entered the world, and my life came crashing down around me—and would soon include a deep and intense bitterness toward God.
>
> I never denied that God existed or is powerful; I concluded he was mean and capricious. But it also began God's work of creating an affection for him and for the sufficiency of Jesus Christ. I am often astonished, when thinking back, that I am now able to praise God for his goodness in giving my son his autism and blindness.
>
> None of this happened easily or by accident. I can point to five specific things that God brought to bear on my life:
>
> 1. Faithful pastoral leadership. I can still remember Pastor Tom Steller . . . walking up my front steps with a note from Pastor John. And I remember sitting with and emailing Pastor David Michael.
>
> These men, with great courage and biblical conviction, entered into dangerous territory. My attorney, a

[8]Available online at http://www.desiringgod.org.

man trained in conflict, said that my intensity and bitterness frightened him. But my pastors never wavered from bringing a message of hope and absolute certainty in the sovereignty and goodness of God, even when I pushed them away.

2. Faithful people of Bethlehem Baptist Church. Shortly after my son was born, we dropped everything at church—our small group, volunteering, Sunday school class, and attendance. One couple refused to let us go and loved us with a gracious, firm, consistent tenderness that made me want to understand how they could love someone like me, my wife, or my son so completely.

3. A faithful father. My own father was the first person in the world to understand and communicate my son's value and inherent worth as a creation of a good and loving God to me. Through 13 years, he has stood with me through much pain and sorrow—and joy.

4. A faithful wife. My wife and I have not walked the same path; hers has been much harder than mine for many reasons. But by the grace of God, we are together, and I thank God every day for this woman whose spine is made of steel and who loves me and our four children.

5. The sovereignty of God as revealed in his word. I remember a particularly heartbroken, bitter email I sent to Pastor John. He had every right

to discipline me, but instead wrapped the words of the Bible around my heart. God used those words from the Bible, among many others, to create longings I didn't have, to start a dead heart beating, and to reveal, when I was incapable of seeing, the beauty, sufficiency, and majesty of Jesus Christ and his cross.

God has done it all, and it was his word that proved decisive.

Living with a boy, now a teenager no less, who will always be dependent on someone for all his needs is hard. I have a daily, often hourly, fight for joy in my salvation. Yet, through my oldest son's daily care, through my youngest son's premature birth, and now through my wife's ongoing battle with metastatic cancer, God is not just sustaining me, but revealing more of his goodness because he is sovereign over all these things, for his glory and my good.

So, on this Independence Day, I am grateful to Jesus for my real freedom in him and for giving me my boy to help me see it: So if the Son sets you free, you will be free indeed (John 8:36).

Happy birthday, Paul.

Seeing is a precious gift. And bitterness is a powerful blindness. What would Naomi say if she could see only a fraction of the thousands of things God was doing in the bitter providences of her life? For example, what if she knew that God was choosing an "unclean" outsider, a Moabitess—just as he chose Rahab the prostitute (Matt. 1:5; Josh. 2:1) and Tamar who played the prostitute (Matt. 1:3; Gen. 38:15)—as the kind of person he wanted in the bloodline of his Son, so that no one could boast in Jewishness—or any other ethnicity? What if she knew that part of what God was doing was shaping a genealogy for the Messiah that would humble the world?

What if she could see that in Ruth she would gain a man-child, and that this man-child would be the grandfather of the greatest king of Israel, and that this king of Israel would be the ancestor of the King of kings, Jesus Christ, the Lord of the universe? If she had trusted God that such things were in the offing, she may have said,

> *Judge not the Lord by feeble sense,*
> *But trust him for his grace;*
> *Behind a frowning providence*
> *He hides a smiling face.*[9]

So the chapter ends with Naomi full of sorrow and with the horizon brightening with hope.

---

[9]Cowper, "God Moves in a Mysterious Way."

Let's draw together some of the lessons of this chapter.

1. God's Sovereign Rule

Naomi got this much right. God the Almighty reigns in all the affairs of men. He rules the affairs of nations (Dan. 2:21) and the flight of birds (Matt. 10:29). His providence extends from the U.S. Congress to your kitchen. Whatever else the great women of faith doubted, they never doubted that God governed every part of their lives and that none could stay his hand (Dan. 4:35).

He gives rain, and he takes rain (Job 38:26; Ps. 147:8). He gives life, and he takes life (Job 1:21). He governs the roll of dice (Prov. 16:33) and the rise of kings (Dan. 2:21). Nothing—from toothpicks to tyrants—is ultimately self-determining. Everything serves (willingly or not) "the purpose of him who works all things according to the counsel of his will" (Eph. 1:11). God is the all-encompassing, all-pervading, all-governing reality.

Naomi was right, and we should join her in this conviction. God the Almighty reigns in all the affairs of men.

2. God's Mysterious Providence

God's providence is sometimes very hard. It's true, God had dealt bitterly with Naomi—at least in the short run, it could only feel like bitterness. Perhaps someone will say, "It was all owing to the sin of going to Moab and marrying foreign wives." Maybe so. But not necessarily.

Psalm 34:19 says, "Many are the afflictions of the righteous, but the LORD delivers him out of them all." Neither the Old Testament nor the New Testament promises that believers will escape affliction in this life. "Through many tribulations we must enter the kingdom of God" (Acts 14:22). "Therefore let those who suffer according to God's will entrust their souls to a faithful Creator" (1 Pet. 4:19). The one who suffered most deserved it least: Jesus Christ. There is no sure connection between our suffering and our behavior. It is not at all certain, therefore, that Naomi's affliction was owing to God's displeasure with her.

But suppose Naomi's calamity was owing to her disobedience. That makes the story doubly encouraging because it shows that God is willing and able even to turn his judgments into joys. If Ruth was brought into the family by sin, it is doubly astonishing that she is made the grandmother of David and ancestor of Jesus Christ. Don't ever think that the sin of your past means there is no hope for your future.

3. God's Good Purposes

That leads to the third lesson. Not only does God reign in all the affairs of men, and not only is his providence sometimes hard, but in all his works his purposes are for the good and the greater happiness of his people. Who would have imagined that in the worst of all times—the period of the judges—God was quietly moving in the tragedies of a single family to prepare the way for the greatest king of Israel?

But not only that, he was working to fill Naomi and Ruth and Boaz and their friends with great joy. If anything painful has fallen on you to make your future look hopeless, learn from Ruth that God is at work for you right now to give you a future and a hope. Trust him. Wait patiently. The ominous clouds are big with mercy and will break with blessing on your head.

4. Freedom and Courage Like Ruth's

Finally, we learn that if you trust the sovereign goodness and mercy of God to pursue you all the days of your life, then you are free for radical love like Ruth's. If God calls, you can leave family, you can leave your job, you can leave your homeland, and you can make risky commitments and undertake new ventures. Or you can find the freedom and courage and strength to keep a commitment you already made.

Mary Slessor's Courage

Mary Slessor (1848–1915) was a courageous missionary to Calabar (Nigeria). She was born in Aberdeen, Scotland, and was converted as a youth. "It was hell-fire that drove her into the Kingdom, she would sometimes say. But once there she found it to be a kingdom of love and tenderness and mercy."[10]

She was given a Bible, and her life changed.

> Most of all it was the story of Christ that she pored over and thought about. His Divine majesty, the beauty and grace of His life, the pathos of His death on the Cross, that affected her inexpressibly. But it was His love, so strong, so tender, so pitiful, that won her heart and devotion and filled her with happiness and peace that suffused her inner life like sunshine. In return she loved Him

[10]W. P. Livingstone, *Mary Slessor of Calabar: Pioneer Missionary* (London: Hodder and Stoughton, 1916), 3.

with a love so intense that it was often a pain. . . .
As the years passed she surrendered herself more
and more to His influence, and was ready for any
duty she was called upon to do for Him, no matter
how humble or exacting it might be. It was this
passion of love and gratitude, this abandonment of
self, this longing for service, that carried her into
her life-work.[11]

Her training for the hardships and dangers of missions
was on the city streets. She volunteered as a teacher in
a mission school. She and others ventured outdoor ministry and were pelted with mud and stones.

There was one gang that was resolved to break up
the mission with which she had come to be identified.
One night they closed in about her on the street. The
leader carried a leaden weight at the end of a piece
of cord, and swung it threateningly around her head.
She stood her ground. Nearer and nearer the missile
came. It shaved her brow. She never winced. The
weight crashed to the ground. "She's game, boys," he
exclaimed. To show their appreciation of her spirit
they went in a body to the meeting. There her bright
eyes, her sympathy, and her firmness shaped them
into order and attention.[12]

[11]Ibid., 8.
[12]Ibid., 9.

When people objected to her going to Calabar, which was called "the white man's grave," she would answer that "Calabar was the post of danger, and was therefore the post of honour."[13]

The reason Mary Slessor could act with courage in the cause of Christ was that she knew herself to be secure under the wings of God. Not that she could not be killed, but that even the hand of death was the hand of Christ.

> I do not like that petition in the Prayer Book, *From sudden death, good Lord, deliver us.* I never could pray it. It is surely far better to see Him at once without pain of parting or physical debility. Why should we not be like the apostle in his confident outburst of praise and assurance, "For I am persuaded . . . " [Acts 26:26]? Don't talk about the *cold* hand of death—it is the hand of Christ.[14]

When you believe in the sovereignty of God and that he loves to work mightily for those who trust him, it gives a freedom and courage that isn't abandoned in hard times. The story of Ruth—and of all the courageous women who followed her—gives us a glimpse into the hidden

[13]Ibid., 18.
[14]Ibid., 324.

work of God during the worst of times. And so like all the other Scriptures, as Paul says (Rom. 15:4, 13), the book of Ruth was written that we might abound in hope—and in that hope live lives of Christ-exalting courage.

5. The Glory of Christ

The ground of our love-releasing hope is not only that in the worst of times God is at work generally for our good, but also that he is working all things specifically for the glory of his Son, Jesus Christ—son of David, son of Jesse, son of Obed, son of Ruth the Moabitess. We "cheated" and read the end of Ruth first. This is where it is all going (Ruth 4:21–22).

And the glory of Christ is supremely the glory of grace. And that grace was shown supremely in the cross where all our sins were covered and all God's promises are secured. Every lasting blessing that came to Ruth and Naomi and Boaz was bought by the blood of Christ a millennium after the blessing was given. Without Christ, sin has no final remission. And where sin has no remission, guilt remains. And where guilt remains, the wrath of God remains. And where the wrath of God remains, there is no lasting blessing, but only everlasting misery.

Therefore, the very wonder of God's gracious providence to make a Moabite an ancestor of Jesus was itself made possible by the death of Jesus for that Moabite on Calvary. The blessings of Christ's blood flow backward and forward in history. "God put [Christ] forward as a propitiation by his blood . . . to show God's righteousness, because in his divine forbearance he had passed over former sins" (Rom. 3:25). In other words, all of Ruth's sins were laid on Jesus when he died. And all of God's wrath toward her was removed. God counted her as righteous because of Christ. Christ was the ground of all the good that she received. And all of it magnifies his glory.

CHAPTER TWO

UNDER THE WINGS OF GOD

The LORD repay you for what you have done,

and a full reward be given you by the LORD,

the God of Israel, under whose wings

you have come to take refuge!

RUTH 2:12

Now Naomi had a relative of her husband's, a worthy man of the clan of Elimelech, whose name was Boaz. [2] And Ruth the Moabite said to Naomi, "Let me go to the field and glean among the ears of grain after him in whose sight I shall find favor." And she said to her, "Go, my daughter." [3] So she set out and went and gleaned in the field after the reapers, and she happened to come to the part of the field belonging to Boaz, who was of the clan of Elimelech. [4] And behold, Boaz came from Bethlehem. And he said to the reapers, "The LORD be with you!" And they answered, "The LORD bless you." [5] Then Boaz said to his young man who was in charge of the reapers, "Whose young woman is this?" [6] And the servant who was in charge of the reapers answered, "She is the young Moabite woman, who came back with Naomi from the country of Moab. [7] She said, 'Please let me glean and gather among the sheaves after the reapers.' So she came, and she has continued from early morning until now, except for a short rest."

[8] Then Boaz said to Ruth, "Now, listen, my daughter, do not go to glean in another field or leave this one, but keep close to my young women. [9] Let your eyes be on the field that they are reaping, and go after them.

Have I not charged the young men not to touch you? And when you are thirsty, go to the vessels and drink what the young men have drawn." [10] *Then she fell on her face, bowing to the ground, and said to him, "Why have I found favor in your eyes, that you should take notice of me, since I am a foreigner?"* [11] *But Boaz answered her, "All that you have done for your mother-in-law since the death of your husband has been fully told to me, and how you left your father and mother and your native land and came to a people that you did not know before.* [12] *The LORD repay you for what you have done, and a full reward be given you by the LORD, the God of Israel, under whose wings you have come to take refuge!"* [13] *Then she said, "I have found favor in your eyes, my lord, for you have comforted me and spoken kindly to your servant, though I am not one of your servants."*

[14] *And at mealtime Boaz said to her, "Come here and eat some bread and dip your morsel in the wine." So she sat beside the reapers, and he passed to her roasted grain. And she ate until she was satisfied, and she had some left over.* [15] *When she rose to glean, Boaz instructed his young men, saying, "Let her glean even among the sheaves, and do not reproach her.* [16] *And also pull out*

some from the bundles for her and leave it for her to glean, and do not rebuke her."

[17] So she gleaned in the field until evening. Then she beat out what she had gleaned, and it was about an ephah of barley. [18] And she took it up and went into the city. Her mother-in-law saw what she had gleaned. She also brought out and gave her what food she had left over after being satisfied. [19] And her mother-in-law said to her, "Where did you glean today? And where have you worked? Blessed be the man who took notice of you." So she told her mother-in-law with whom she had worked and said, "The man's name with whom I worked today is Boaz." [20] And Naomi said to her daughter-in-law, "May he be blessed by the LORD, whose kindness has not forsaken the living or the dead!" Naomi also said to her, "The man is a close relative of ours, one of our redeemers." [21] And Ruth the Moabite said, "Besides, he said to me, 'You shall keep close by my young men until they have finished all my harvest.'" [22] And Naomi said to Ruth, her daughter-in-law, "It is good, my daughter, that you go out with his young women, lest in another field you be assaulted." [23] So she kept close to the young women of Boaz, gleaning until the end of the barley

and wheat harvests. And she lived with her mother-in-law. (Ruth 2)

THE HAND OF GOD HAD FALLEN hard upon Naomi and her family—a famine in Judah, a move to Moab, the death of her husband, the marriage of her sons to foreign wives, ten years of apparent childlessness for both daughters-in-law, then the death of her sons, and the departure of one of her daughters-in-law. One blow after another caused Naomi to say, "The hand of the LORD has gone out against me. . . . The Almighty has dealt very bitterly with me" (1:13, 20).

In fact, she is so oppressed by God's bitter providence in her life that she can't see the signs of hope as they start to appear. She knows there is a God. She knows he is sovereign and rules over the national and personal affairs of men. And she knows that God has dealt bitterly with her. Her life is tragic. What she does not see with the eyes of her heart is that in all her bitter experiences, God is plotting for her glory. This is true of all God's children. In the darkest of our times, God is plotting for our glory. If we would believe this and remember it, we would not be as blind as Naomi was when God began to reveal his grace.

Sweet Providence Unseen

Sweet providence, as well as bitter, came to Naomi. God lifted the famine and opened a way home. He gave her an amazingly devoted and loving daughter-in-law to accompany her. And he preserved a kinsman of Naomi's husband who would someday marry Ruth and preserve Naomi's line.

But Naomi appears unmoved from her sorrows by any of this merciful providence. When she returned to Bethlehem, she said to the townspeople, "I went away full, and the LORD has brought me back empty. Why call me Naomi, when the LORD has testified against me and the Almighty has brought calamity upon me?" (1:21). So Ruth and bitter Naomi settle in Bethlehem. In the second chapter of Ruth, the mercy of God becomes so obvious that even Naomi will recognize it.

In verses 1–7, we meet Boaz, we see the character of Ruth, and we sense a very merciful providence behind this scene.

A God-Saturated Man

Boaz, we learn, is a relative of Elimelech, Naomi's long-deceased husband. Immediately we realize that things are not nearly as bleak as Naomi said they were back in 1:11–13 when she gave the impression that there was no one for Ruth and Orpah to marry to carry on the line of their husbands. For the person reading this story the first time, Boaz is like a bright crack in the cloud of bitterness hanging over Naomi. It's going to get bigger and bigger.

For example, 2:1 says that Boaz is "a worthy man." The Hebrew phrase for "worthy man" is also translated "man of valor" (1 Sam. 16:18), "mighty man" (1 Chron. 28:1), "man of wealth" (1 Sam. 9:1), and "very able" (1 Kings 11:28). It is a broad commendation of Boaz's strength and ability and courage and success. He is an admirable man.

But more important than his reputation, he is a man of God. We see this in Ruth 2:4 where the author pauses to record an incidental detail; he tells us how Boaz greeted his servants. "And behold, Boaz came from Bethlehem. And he said to the reapers, 'The LORD be with you!' And they answered, 'The LORD bless you.'" If you want to know a man's relation to God, it helps to find out how far God has saturated him down to the details of his everyday life. Evidently Boaz was such a God-saturated man that his farming business and his relationships to his employees was shot through with

God. He greeted them with God. And we will see that these were more than pious platitudes.

A Woman of Initiative, Lowliness, and Industry

Besides meeting Boaz in verses 1–7, we also see the qualities of Ruth's character, which will be crucial in what this chapter intends to teach.

First, she took the initiative to care for her mother-in-law. Naomi does not command Ruth to get out and work. Ruth says, "Let me go to the field and glean among the ears of grain" (2:2). Ruth has committed herself to Naomi with amazing devotion, and she takes the initiative to work and provide for her.

Second, Ruth is humble. She knows how to take initiative without being presumptuous. The servants report to Boaz how she had approached them that morning. She had said, "Please let me glean and gather among the sheaves after the reapers" (2:7). She does not demand a handout. She does not presume the right even to glean at the edges of the field. All she wants to do is gather up the leftovers after the reapers are done, and she asks permission even to do that. She is like another foreign woman who came to Jesus and said, "Yes, Lord, yet even the dogs eat the crumbs that fall from their masters' table" (Matt. 15:27). To this Jesus responded by commending her faith. Ruth knows how to take initiative, but she is not pushy or presumptuous but meek and humble.

Third, she is industrious. She is an amazing worker. Boaz's servants tell him, "She has continued from early morning until now, except for a short rest" (Ruth 2:7). Verse 17 goes on to say that she gleaned until evening, and then before she quit, she beat out what she gleaned, measured it, and took it home to Naomi.

There is no doubt that the writer wants us to admire and imitate Ruth. She takes initiative to care for her destitute mother-in-law. She is humble and meek and does not put herself forward presumptuously. And she works hard from sunup to sundown. Initiative. Lowliness. Industry. Worthy traits. We will see them again.

"She Happened to Come"

But before we leave Ruth 2:1–7, did you sense a merciful providence behind all this? Notice verse 3: "So she set out and went and gleaned in the field after the reapers, and she happened to come to the part of the field belonging to Boaz, who was of the clan of Elimelech." She just "happened to come"?

You don't have to make your theology of providence explicit in every line. Sometimes it's good to leave something ambiguous to give your reader a chance to fill in the blank if he has caught on. The answer can be given later. It will be. In fact, Naomi, with her grand theology of God's sovereignty, is the one who will give the answer. She praises the Lord "whose kindness has not forsaken the living or the dead!" (2:20). The answer is God—the merciful providence of God—guiding Ruth as she gleans. Ruth *happened to come* to Boaz's field because God is gracious and sovereign even when he is silent. "A man's steps are from the LORD; how then can man understand his way?" (Prov. 20:24).

Now Boaz approaches Ruth and shows her great kindness, even though she is a foreigner. He provides food by telling her to work in his field and stay close behind his maidens (Ruth 2:8). He provides protection by telling the young men not to molest her. And he provides for her thirst by telling her to drink from what the men have drawn (2:9). So all of Boaz's wealth and godliness begin to turn for Ruth's welfare.

"Why Have I Found Favor in Your Sight?"

Now we come to the most important interchange in the chapter—verses 10–13. Ruth raises a question to Boaz that turns out to be very profound. It's one that we all need to ask God. Hardly anything in our life is more important than the answer we get.

"Then she fell on her face, bowing to the ground, and said to him, 'Why have I found favor in your eyes, that you should take notice of me, since I am a foreigner?'" (2:10). Ruth knows that she is a Moabitess. From a natural viewpoint, she is at a great disadvantage; she is a foreigner. She does not resent this but accepts it. As a non-Israelite, she does not expect any special treatment. Her response to Boaz's kindness is humble astonishment.

She is different from most people today. We have a sense of entitlement. We expect kindness and are astonished and resentful if we don't get our "rights." But Ruth expresses her sense of unworthiness by falling on her face and bowing to the ground. Proud people don't feel amazed at being treated well. They don't feel deep gratefulness. But humble people do. In fact, they are made even more humble by being treated graciously. They are so amazed that grace came to them in their unworthiness that they feel even more lowly. But they receive the gift. Joy increases, not self-importance. Grace is not intended to replace lowliness with pride. It's intended to replace sorrow with joy.

"Because You Took Refuge under the Wings of God"

But we're getting ahead of ourselves. Ruth asks why Boaz has treated her so graciously—or why God had ordained for Boaz to be so gracious. "Why have I found favor in your eyes, that you should take notice of me, since I am a foreigner?" (2:10). Boaz's answer is crucial to this chapter, indeed to the rest of the book:

> But Boaz answered her, "All that you have done for your mother-in-law since the death of your husband has been fully told to me, and how you left your father and mother and your native land and came to a people that you did not know before. The LORD repay you for what you have done, and a full reward be given you by the LORD, the God of Israel, under whose wings you have come to take refuge!" (2:11–12)

Notice: When Ruth asks why she is being shown grace, Boaz does not answer that this grace has no conditions.

He answers her question *Why?* by saying, "Because you have loved Naomi so much that you were willing to leave father and mother to serve her in a strange land."

Does this mean that the writer wants us to think of Ruth's love for Naomi as a work that merits Boaz's favor and the favor of God? Does he want us to think of grace as a kindness we earn? I don't think so. If Ruth has earned the favor of Boaz (and of God), then we must think of her as a kind of employee rendering service to her employer—a service that is so valuable that he is indebted to pay her. She merits the pay. That's not the image the writer wants to create in our minds. Verse 12 gives another image that makes the employer-employee image impossible.

Boaz says in verse 12 that God is really the one who is rewarding Ruth for her love to Naomi. Boaz is only the instrument of God—as we will learn from Naomi in just a moment. But now notice the words, "The LORD repay you for what you have done, and a full reward be given you by the LORD, the God of Israel, under whose wings you have come to take refuge!" In spite of the word "repay" (which could be translated "reward" or "recompense"), this verse does not encourage us to picture Ruth as an employee of God providing needed labor that he then as employer rewards with a good wage. The picture is of God as a great winged Eagle and Ruth as a threatened little eaglet coming to find safety under the Eagle's wings. The implication of verse 12 is that God will reward Ruth because she has sought refuge under his wings.

How God Upholds the Worth of His Name

This is a common teaching in the Old Testament. For example, Psalm 57:1 says, "Be merciful to me, O God, be merciful to me, for in you my soul takes refuge; in the shadow of your wings I will take refuge." Notice the word *for*. "Be merciful to me, *for* in you my soul takes refuge." Why should God show mercy to Ruth? Because she has sought refuge under his wings.

She has esteemed God's protection superior to all others. She has set her heart on God for hope and joy. And when a person does that, God's honor—not the value of our work—is at stake, and he will be merciful. If you plead God's value as the source of your hope instead of pleading your value as a reason for God's blessing, then his unwavering commitment to his own glory engages all his heart for your protection and joy.

Boaz prayed that God would reward Ruth for all that she had done for her mother-in-law. "A full reward be given you by the LORD, the God of Israel, under whose wings you have come to take refuge!" (Ruth 2:12). Now we see that this "reward" is not a kind of justification by works or salvation by merit. We see that the way God works is to bless those who hope in his work for them, not their work for him. "His delight is not in the strength of the horse, nor his pleasure in the legs of a man, but the LORD takes pleasure in those . . . who hope in his steadfast love" (Ps. 147:10–11).

The reason God acts this way is that his righteousness commits him to uphold the worth of his name. So when we come to him pleading the worth of his name, not ours, he helps us. "For your name's sake, O LORD, pardon my guilt, for it is great" (Ps. 25:11). Pardon and blessing come to those who look away from their own worth to the worth of God's name. It is God's righteousness to stand by his name. "For your name's sake, O LORD, preserve my life! In your righteousness bring my soul out of trouble!" (Ps. 143:11).

Therefore, we are hearing something very profound when we hear Boaz say, in effect, "Ruth, because you have come to take refuge under the wings of God, therefore I pray he will vindicate the power and grace of his wings and give you what you need."

Where the Eagle Moves I Will Move

But we must ask how Ruth's love for Naomi and her leaving her own family relate to her seeking refuge under the wings of God. The most likely suggestion is that Ruth was able to leave the refuge of her father and mother in Moab because she had found a far superior refuge—under the wings of God. And evidently she saw a need in Naomi's life and sensed God's calling to meet that need. The Eagle moved toward Naomi, and in order to keep enjoying the refuge of God's wings, Ruth moves, too, and commits herself to care for Naomi with the care she is receiving from God.

How the Christian Life Works

This is the way the Christian life is meant to work. Peter and Paul say it in their own unique ways. Peter says, "Whoever serves, [let him serve] as one who serves by the strength that God supplies—in order that in everything God may be glorified through Jesus Christ" (1 Pet. 4:11). We take refuge under the wings of God and get our strength from him. And with that strength we serve others (as Ruth served Naomi). God responds to this kind of "faith working through love" (Gal. 5:6) because in this way he is glorified.

Similarly, Paul says, "By the grace of God I am what I am, and his grace toward me was not in vain. On the contrary, I worked harder than any of them, though it was not I, but the grace of God that is with me" (1 Cor. 15:10). Paul worked hard, just as Ruth worked hard from sunup to sundown. But he worked in God's strength. He had come under the wings of God and was getting his strength from him. Paul did not earn God's grace with his hard work. Grace made his hard work possible. That's the way it was with Ruth. Boaz does not mean that she will find favor with God because of her work. Rather, she found favor with God by coming under his wings as an undeserving Moabitess. And in the strength of that favor she was working.

The Source of Risk-Taking Love

So the relation between taking refuge under God's wings, on the one hand, and leaving home to care for Naomi, on the other hand, is that being under God's wings enabled Ruth to forsake human refuge and give herself in love to Naomi. Or another way to say it is that leaving home and loving Naomi are the result and evidence of taking refuge in God. This is why I said in the introduction that one of the aims of this book is to release radical, risk-taking love. It comes from humble confidence in the mighty and merciful wings of God.

So now back to Ruth's question in Ruth 2:10: "Why have I found favor?" The answer is that she has taken refuge under the wings of God and that this has given her the freedom and the desire to leave home and love Naomi. She has not earned mercy from God or Boaz. She is not their employee. They are not paying her wages for her work. On the contrary, she has honored them by admitting her need for their work and by taking refuge in their generosity.

No "Help Wanted"

This is the message of the biblical gospel. God will have mercy on anyone (Palestinian or Israelite or American) who humbles himself, like Ruth, and takes refuge under the wings of God. Jesus said,

> O Jerusalem, Jerusalem, the city that kills the prophets and stones those who are sent to it! How often would I have gathered your children together as a hen gathers her brood under her wings, and you would not! Behold, your house is forsaken. (Luke 13:34–35)

All the Pharisees had to do was to take refuge under the

wings of Jesus. Stop trying to justify themselves (Luke 10:29; 16:15; 18:9). Stop relying on themselves. Stop glorifying themselves. But they would not. Ruth was not their model. No falling on their faces before Jesus. No bowing down. No astonishment at grace. Don't be like the Pharisees. Be like Ruth.

While jogging in my neighborhood, I used to see a graphic illustration of this difference. For several years, as I ran east on Franklin Avenue and then south on Cedar, I would pass a tool-and-die shop. There was a permanent "help wanted" sign bolted above the door. But almost every time I ran by, a big red "NO" was fastened on top of "help wanted." Every time I saw it, I rejoiced in this picture of the gospel. The good news is that God does not need our help. The gospel is not an employment ad.

God is not an employer looking for employees. He is an Eagle looking for people who will take refuge under his wings. He is looking for people who will leave father and mother and homeland or anything else that may hold them back from a life of love under the wings of Jesus.

Awakening to the Kindness of God

Let's close this chapter by getting back to Naomi briefly. Boaz gives Ruth all she can eat for lunch (Ruth 2:14). She works till sundown. She returns to Naomi and gives her the leftovers from lunch and all the grain. She tells her what happened with Boaz (2:17–19). At this point, Naomi's theology of God's sovereignty serves her well.

She says, "May he be blessed by the LORD, whose kindness has not forsaken the living or the dead!" (2:20). Whose kindness is she praising? Boaz's or the Lord's? Surely, she is praising the Lord's kindness. Boaz had just begun to show kindness to the dead. It was God who seemed to have forsaken it. But the Lord's kindness has not forsaken the living (Naomi and Ruth) or the dead (Elimelech and Mahlon and Chilion).

It was the Lord who stopped the famine. It was the Lord who bound Ruth to Naomi in love. It was the Lord who preserved Boaz for Ruth. It was no coincidence that Ruth happened to come to Boaz's field. It was no coincidence that Boaz happened to show favor to this poor foreigner. The Lord directed her steps and his favor. The light of God's love has finally broken through bright enough for Naomi to see. The Lord is kind. He is good to all who take refuge under his wings.

With Ruth and Naomi, let us fall on our faces, bow before the Lord, confess our unworthiness, take refuge under the wings of God, and be astonished at his grace.

CHAPTER THREE

STRATEGIC RIGHTEOUSNESS

And now, my daughter, do not fear.
I will do for you all that you ask,
for all my fellow townsmen know that you
are a worthy woman.

RUTH 3:11

*T*hen Naomi her mother-in-law said to her, "My daughter, should I not seek rest for you, that it may be well with you? ² Is not Boaz our relative, with whose young women you were? See, he is winnowing barley tonight at the threshing floor. ³ Wash therefore and anoint yourself, and put on your cloak and go down to the threshing floor, but do not make yourself known to the man until he has finished eating and drinking. ⁴ But when he lies down, observe the place where he lies. Then go and uncover his feet and lie down, and he will tell you what to do." ⁵ And she replied, "All that you say I will do."

⁶ So she went down to the threshing floor and did just as her mother-in-law had commanded her. ⁷ And when Boaz had eaten and drunk, and his heart was merry, he went to lie down at the end of the heap of grain. Then she came softly and uncovered his feet and lay down. ⁸ At midnight the man was startled and turned over, and behold, a woman lay at his feet! ⁹ He said, "Who are you?" And she answered, "I am Ruth, your servant. Spread your wings over your servant, for you are a redeemer." ¹⁰ And he said, "May you be blessed by the LORD, my daughter. You have made this last kindness greater than the first in that

you have not gone after young men, whether poor or rich. [11] And now, my daughter, do not fear. I will do for you all that you ask, for all my fellow townsmen know that you are a worthy woman. [12] And now it is true that I am a redeemer. Yet there is a redeemer nearer than I. [13] Remain tonight, and in the morning, if he will redeem you, good; let him do it. But if he is not willing to redeem you, then, as the LORD lives, I will redeem you. Lie down until the morning."

[14] So she lay at his feet until the morning, but arose before one could recognize another. And he said, "Let it not be known that the woman came to the threshing floor." [15] And he said, "Bring the garment you are wearing and hold it out." So she held it, and he measured out six measures of barley and put it on her. Then she went into the city. [16] And when she came to her mother-in-law, she said, "How did you fare, my daughter?" Then she told her all that the man had done for her, [17] saying, "These six measures of barley he gave to me, for he said to me, 'You must not go back empty-handed to your mother-in-law.'" [18] She replied, "Wait, my daughter, until you learn how the matter turns out, for the man will not rest but will settle the matter today." (Ruth 3)

The Clouds Are Big with Mercy

The story of Ruth began with the bitter providence of
God in the life of Naomi as she left her land and lost her
husband, her sons, and one of her daughters-in-law. But
there was sweet providence as well. The famine broke
in Judah, and Naomi could go home. Ruth committed
herself to care for Naomi. And all the while, a kinsman
named Boaz was preserved as a husband for Ruth to
raise up an heir for the family name. But the first chapter ends with Naomi overwhelmed with her losses: "The
Almighty has dealt very bitterly with me" (1:20).

In chapter 2, the mercy of God breaks through bright
enough for even Naomi to see it. We meet Boaz, a man of
worth, a man of God, and a relative of Naomi's husband.
We see Ruth taking refuge under the wings of God in a
foreign land and being led mercifully by God to the field
of Boaz to glean. And we see Naomi recover from her long
night of despondency as she exults in God: "[The Lord's]
kindness has not forsaken the living or the dead!" (2:20).

Chapter 2 overflows with hope. Boaz is a God-
saturated man in his business and personal relations
(2:4, 10–13). Ruth is a God-dependent woman under the
wings of God. Naomi is now a God-exalting woman under
the sovereignty of God. All the darkness of chapter 1 is

gone. God has turned her mourning into dancing. "The Almighty has dealt very bitterly with me" (1:20) has given way to his "kindness has not forsaken the living or the dead!" (2:20). The lesson so far is surely at least this:

> *You fearful saints, fresh courage take:*
> *The clouds you so much dread*
> *Are big with mercy and will break*
> *In blessings on your head.*[1]

Seek refuge under the wings of God, even when they seem to cast only shadows, and at just the right time God will let you look out from his Eagle's nest onto some spectacular sunrise.

Hope: The Birthplace of Dreams

As we turn to chapter 3, keep in mind the phrase *strategic righteousness*. The question this chapter answers is, *What do a God-saturated man, a God-dependent young woman, and a God-exalting older woman do when they are filled with hope in the sovereign goodness of God?* The answer is that they manifest what I am going to call *strategic righteousness*.

By *righteousness* I mean a zeal for doing what is good and right—a zeal for doing what is fitting when

[1] William Cowper, "God Moves in a Mysterious Way" (1774).

God is taken into account as sovereign and merciful. By *strategic* I mean that there is intention, purposefulness, planning. There is a kind of inactive righteousness that simply avoids evil. But *strategic righteousness* takes the initiative and dreams of how to make things right.

One of the lessons I have learned from this chapter is that hope helps us dream. Hope helps us think up ways to do good. Hope helps us pursue our ventures with virtue and integrity. It's hopelessness that makes people think they have to lie and steal and seize illicit pleasures for the moment. But hope, based on the confidence that a sovereign God is for us, gives us a thrilling impulse that I call *strategic righteousness*. We see it in Naomi in 3:1–5, in Ruth in 3:6–9, and in Boaz in 3:10–15. And the chapter closes again with Naomi full of confidence in the power and goodness of God.

The Offspring of Naomi's Hope

Two things stand out in Naomi's strategy in 3:1–5. One is that she has a strategy; and the other is what that strategy is.

The sheer fact that Naomi has a strategy teaches us something. People who are depressed because they are victims rarely make plans. This is true whether they are real victims of wrongdoing or only feel like they are. We live in a time when this distinction is important. Feeling hurt does not necessarily mean someone has wronged us. God certainly disciplines his people with pain, but he never wrongs them (Heb. 12:3–11). In other words, feeling hurt by others, and being a victim are not always the same. Nevertheless, it is possible to be depressed by either—by being victims of real wrong or by only feeling wronged when we are not. Naomi's response to God's providence was, at first, hopelessness. As long as Naomi felt only oppressed—as long as she could only say, "The Almighty has dealt very bitterly with me"—she conceived no strategy for the future.

One of the terrible effects of depression is the inability to move purposefully and hopefully into the future. Strategies of righteousness are the overflow of hope. When Naomi awakens in 2:20 to the kindness of God, her hope comes alive, and the overflow is strategic righteousness. She is concerned about finding Ruth a place of provision and protection. She makes a plan.

One of the reasons we must help each other "hope in God" (Ps. 42:5) is that only hopeful people, hopeful families, and hopeful churches plan and strategize. I always felt a special calling to impart hope to the church I served. Churches that feel no hope develop a maintenance mentality and just go through the motions year in and year out. But when a church feels the sovereign kindness of God hovering overhead and moving, hope starts to thrive, and righteousness ceases to be simply the avoidance of evil and becomes active and strategic.

Naomi takes the initiative to find a husband for Ruth. But the strategy she comes up with is odd, to say the least. She says that Boaz is a relative (3:2), and therefore he is the likely candidate for being Ruth's husband—that way the family name and family inheritance will stay in the family, according to Hebrew custom.

The Incredible Plan

So Naomi's aim is clear: to win for Ruth a godly husband and a secure future and preserve the family line. So she tells Ruth to make herself as clean and attractive as possible, go to the threshing floor of Boaz, and after he has lain down for the evening, sneak in, lift up his cloak, and lie down at his feet. Everybody, including Ruth, must respond by thinking, "And just where do you suppose that will lead?" To which Naomi gives the extraordinary answer, "He will tell you what to do" (3:4).

One thing is clear here, and one thing is not. It's clear that this is Naomi's way of trying to get Boaz to marry Ruth. It is not clear why she should go about it like this. Why not a conversation with Boaz instead of this highly suggestive and risky midnight maneuver? Was Naomi indifferent to the possibility that Boaz might drive Ruth away in moral indignation, or that he might give in to the temptation to have sexual relations with her? Did Naomi want that to happen? Or was Naomi so sure of Boaz and Ruth that she knew they would treat each other with perfect purity—that Boaz would be deeply moved by this outright offer of Ruth in marriage and would avoid sexual relations until all was duly solemnized by the city elders?

The author doesn't come right out and tell us why Naomi chose this sexually tempting strategy to win Boaz for Ruth. There will be a clue later, but for now the writer seems to want us to feel suspense and ambiguity. Just where did Ruth lie down? "When he lies down, observe the place where he lies. Then go and uncover his feet and lie down" (3:4). The Hebrew is just as ambiguous as the English. Perpendicular? Parallel? Overlapping?

"And he will tell you what to do" (3:4). Yes. But what would Boaz tell her to do? Whatever Naomi's motive was, the situation is one that could lead us into a passionate and illicit scene of sexual intercourse, or into a stunning scene of purity, integrity, and self-control.

Ruth's Righteous Risk

Next we see Ruth's strategic righteousness in verses 6–9. Ruth said that she would follow all of Naomi's instructions. "All that you say I will do" (3:5). But Ruth does more. Naomi had said that Boaz would tell Ruth what to do. Before that happens, Ruth tells Boaz why she has come. She is lying at his feet under his cloak. He awakes and says, "Who are you?" She answers with words unprompted by Naomi, "I am Ruth, your servant. Spread your wings[2] over your servant, for you are a redeemer" (3:9).

Ruth is not merely Naomi's pawn. She has gone willingly, and now she takes the initiative to make clear to Boaz why she is there. "You are next of kin." Or literally, "You are the redeemer: the one who can redeem our inheritance and our family name from being lost. I want you to fill that role for me. I want to be your wife." She doesn't say it outright. In fact, she is less direct and more enticing. She says, "Spread your wings over your servant." Now whether Boaz takes this to be an offer of outright sexual relations or something more subtle and profound will depend on his

---

[2]This is a literal and very helpful translation, as we will see. Other versions translate it loosely as "spread the corner of your garment over me" (NIV); or "spread therefore thy skirt over thine handmaid" (KJV); or "spread your covering over your maid" (NASB). The word is literally "wings" and usually, in combination with "spreads," refers to what birds do with their wings (Deut. 32:11; Jer. 48:40; 49:22; Job 39:26). The reason the word "wings" is so important to preserve is the connection with Ruth 2:12: "The LORD repay you for what you have done, and a full reward be given you by the LORD, the God of Israel, under whose *wings* you have come to take refuge!"

estimate of Ruth's character. Fornication was wrong in the Old Testament (Lev. 19:29; Deut. 22:13–21), just as in the New Testament (Matt. 15:19).

"You Became Mine"

Two things, besides Ruth's character, suggest something subtle and profound—not immoral—is in fact going on here. One is this: the only other place in the Old Testament where the phrase "spreading the wings" occurs in relation to lovers is found in Ezekiel 16:8. God is describing Israel as a young maiden whom he took for his wife. "When I passed by you again and saw you, behold, you were at the age for love, and I spread the corner of my garment over you [literally, "spread my wings over you"] and covered your nakedness; I made my vow to you and entered into a covenant with you, declares the LORD God, and you became mine." If this is any indication of what Ruth wanted from Boaz, the request went far beyond sexual relations. She was saying in effect, "I would like to be the one to whom you pledge your faithfulness and with whom you make a marriage covenant."

"Spread Your Wings over Me"

But there is more to it than that—and this is the second indication of subtlety and depth here. When Ruth said, "Spread your wings over your servant," the word for "wings" in Hebrew is the same word that Boaz had used back in Ruth 2:12. This was the key phrase we focused on in the previous chapter. Boaz says to Ruth, "The LORD repay you for what you have done, and a full reward be given you by the LORD, the God of Israel, under whose *wings* you have come to take refuge!" What we saw was that Boaz was God's agent to reward Ruth. He gave her free access to his field and protection from the young men and water from the well. Ruth had said to Boaz, "Why have I found favor in your eyes?" And Boaz answered, "Because you have come to take refuge under the wings of God."

What then is going on in chapter 3? Here's my suggestion. Ruth has told Naomi about these words of Boaz. And the more they ponder them, the more they become convinced that they are laden with subtle loving intentions. What Boaz really means is, "Because you take refuge under the wings of God, you are the kind of woman I want to cover with my wings."

It is not easy for an older man to express love to a younger woman. It would be doubly humiliating if she declined—both because he is a man and because he presumed to think a younger woman would be interested in him. Boaz did it with deeds of kindness and subtle words of admiration. He said he admired her for coming under God's wings. He acted as though she were under his, and he waited.

A Subtle Way of Saying Yes

In the course of time, Naomi and Ruth hit upon a response just as subtle, just as profound. Ruth will come to him in his sleep, in the grain field where he has taken her under his care, and she will say yes. But she will say it with an action just as subtle as the action and words of Boaz. She puts herself under his wing, so to speak, and when he wakes, everything hangs on one sentence and whether Ruth has interpreted Boaz correctly.

I imagine her pulse racing as Boaz awoke. Then come the all-important words: "I am Ruth. . . . Spread your wing over your maidservant." I picture an immense silence for a moment while Boaz let himself believe that this magnificent woman had really understood—had so profoundly and sensitively understood. A middle-aged man[3] is interested in a young widow whom he discreetly calls "my daughter" (2:8; 3:10–11), uncertain whether her heart might be going after the younger men, communicating with a subtle word picture that he wants to be God's wings for her. Then a young widow gradually reads between the lines and finally risks

[3] We know Boaz is older because he says to Ruth, "You have not gone after young men" (Ruth 3:10).

an interpretation by coming in the middle of the night to take refuge under the wing of his garment. That's powerful stuff! Anybody who thinks that a loose woman and a finagling mother-in-law are at work here is missing something beautiful. All is subtle. All is righteous. All is strategic.

Sex Will Be Subordinate to Strategic Righteousness

Now comes the strategic righteousness of Boaz in 3:10–15. To hear what he says in the right way, you have to remember that it is midnight, they are under the stars, and he is looking down into the face of the woman he desires, covered with his own cloak next to his feet.

> And he said, "May you be blessed by the LORD, my daughter. You have made this last kindness greater than the first in that you have not gone after young men, whether poor or rich. And now, my daughter, do not fear. I will do for you all that you ask, for all my fellow townsmen know that you are a worthy woman." (3:10–11)

And then comes a word of magnificent righteousness and self-control. He says in effect, "According to custom, Ruth, there is another who has prior claim to you, and I won't be able to proceed until all things are duly settled with him."

> And now it is true that I am a redeemer. Yet there is a redeemer nearer than I. Remain tonight, and in the

> morning, if he will redeem you, good; let him do it. But if
> he is not willing to redeem you, then, as the LORD lives, I
> will redeem you. Lie down until the morning. (3:12–13)

The stars are beautiful overhead, it is midnight, he desires her, she desires him, they are alone, she is under his cloak.

Was their desire pure? Was it sinful? The book of Ruth is portraying them as morally exemplary (2:1; 3:11). What then is the difference between pure and impure sexual desire?

Part of the answer is that it is impure to desire what is impure. But to desire what is pure is pure. Sexual relations in marriage is not impure. It could be made impure by abusive or unloving attitudes or actions. But marital sex in itself is by God's design honorable and joyfully pure (Heb. 13:4; 1 Cor. 7:2–5; Song of Solomon). Therefore to desire it is not in itself impure. I assume that is what Boaz and Ruth felt. They desired to be joined sexually. And they desired it in marriage.

If they had desired sexual relations *with no limitations*, then they would have been guilty of Jesus's future rebuke, "You have heard that it was said, 'You shall not commit adultery.' But I say to you that everyone who looks at a woman to desire her has already committed adultery with her in his heart" (Matt. 5:27–28). This does not mean that desire for marital sex is wrong. God created this desire for the pleasure and fruitfulness of his people (Song 7:10). It means that to desire the kind of sex that God forbids is forbidden.

Ruth and Boaz were strong. They were not enslaved to their desires. Their desires were great and greatly governed by God-given commitments. They sent their culturally appropriate and provocative signals. This is what we want. Then they enclosed those desires in righteousness and stored them up for a God-given day of even greater pleasure (Ruth 3:7–14). This a man and a woman of great character!

Let the Morning Dawn on Your Purity

The mood of American life today is, *If it feels good, do it, and away with guilt-producing, puritanical principles of chastity and faithfulness*. But I say to you who are unmarried, if the stars are shining in their beauty, and your blood is thudding like a hammer, and you are safe in the privacy of your place, stop . . . for the sake of righteousness. Let the morning dawn on your purity.

I close this chapter by pleading with you to stand with Boaz and Ruth in your commitment never to have sexual relations outside of marriage. I know that many of you have already failed. There is hope for forgiveness.

When the apostle Paul described the Christians in Corinth, he included the "sexually immoral," "adulterers," "men who practice homosexuality," along with the thieves and greedy and drunkards and swindlers. But then he said, "Such were some of you. But you were washed, you were sanctified, you were justified in the name of the Lord Jesus Christ and by the Spirit of our God" (1 Cor. 6:9–11). If you have failed sexually, there is forgiveness and cleansing in the offspring of Ruth and Boaz—Jesus Christ.

But for those who have not yet had sexual relations outside marriage—indeed for all who hope to fight for future holiness—I am pleading with you, for your own sake and for the glory of Christ, that you embrace the strategic righteousness of Ruth and Boaz. They are models of deep, strong, righteous, passionate love—better models than politicians and movie stars.

The Purity of the Moment and the Purposes of Eternity

Let's put that night in a larger context. What's happening in this phenomenal triumph of purity is the making of the ancestor of Jesus. Ruth is about to be folded purely and righteously by Boaz into a line that will give birth to Jesus Christ. The purity of the moment and the purposes of eternity come together at this holy moment. Don't miss this. It is relevant for you and your sexual life.

Perhaps you are there in the seeming seclusion and safety of your apartment or on the road where no one knows you. Perhaps she seems so willing. She may already be in your bed. At that moment, a magnificent act of righteous manhood is possible. Say to her, "Because I love you, and because I love God, and because I have seen the connection between high purity and historic purposes, we will wait."

I promise you, God will honor that. He will honor it more vastly than you can imagine. God honored the strategic righteousness of Boaz and Ruth with the last chapter of the story. It culminates in the promise of a coming king through Boaz and a Moabite. "Boaz fathered Obed, Obed fathered Jesse, and Jesse fathered David," and David fathered the Messiah, Jesus Christ (Ruth 4:21–22; Matt. 22:41–46).

Let the beautiful righteousness of Naomi's risky plan awaken your creativity in the cause of purity. Let Ruth's sensitive discernment of this older man's heart deepen your wisdom in the high duties of life. Let Boaz's massive willpower in the service of strategic righteousness stir up in you a great, noble vision of sexual life: "We will wait. We will wait till all is made righteous according to the word of God."

The sexual temptations of our day are pervasive and

powerful, just like they were that night in Bethlehem. Well, maybe not "just like" that night. There is a difference between inevitable desire and intentional seduction. Ruth was not seducing Boaz. But she was creating a situation where their desires were made known and felt. The very fact of a loved woman nearby at night is sexually awakening. "My beloved put his hand to the latch, and my heart was thrilled within me" (Song 5:4). But there is a world of difference between the awakening of desire and the enticement to sin.

There is both similarity and difference between today's sexual temptations and what happened that night on the threshing floor in Bethlehem. The similarity makes the night relevant. The difference makes it a beautiful alternative to sin. And remember, this was Bethlehem. Think of it! Perhaps this triumph of purity took place near the very spot where, a thousand years later, a virgin would give birth to Jesus, the son of David, the son of Jesse, the son of Obed, the son of a pure union between Boaz and Ruth.

"I Know Where I Am Standing"

When you hear the ridicule of those who think you are crazy for not having sex outside of marriage, imagine Boaz and Ruth looking down from heaven in their massively strong and holy manhood and womanhood, glorified in strength and courage and righteousness and purposefulness. Then say to those who ridicule you, "No. I know where I am standing. I know what life is about. I know how purity relates to the grand purposes of God. I know the roots and the righteousness of Jesus Christ. I am going to wait."

And if waiting means never having sexual relations in this life, then set your face to be among the number who join Jesus Christ in that hall of fame. He never had sex. But he is the most fully human person who has ever existed.

Don't be like the world. Be like Boaz. Be like Ruth. Profound in love. Subtle and perceptive in communication. Powerful in self-control. Committed to strategic righteousness.

CHAPTER FOUR

MAY MY REDEEMER
BE RENOWNED

*Blessed be the L*ORD*, who has not left you*

this day without a redeemer, and

may his name be renowned in Israel!

RUTH 4:14

*N*ow *Boaz had gone up to the gate and sat down there. And behold, the redeemer, of whom Boaz had spoken, came by. So Boaz said, "Turn aside, friend; sit down here." And he turned aside and sat down. ² And he took ten men of the elders of the city and said, "Sit down here." So they sat down. ³ Then he said to the redeemer, "Naomi, who has come back from the country of Moab, is selling the parcel of land that belonged to our relative Elimelech. ⁴ So I thought I would tell you of it and say, 'Buy it in the presence of those sitting here and in the presence of the elders of my people.' If you will redeem it, redeem it. But if you will not, tell me, that I may know, for there is no one besides you to redeem it, and I come after you." And he said, "I will redeem it." ⁵ Then Boaz said, "The day you buy the field from the hand of Naomi, you also acquire Ruth the Moabite, the widow of the dead, in order to perpetuate the name of the dead in his inheritance." ⁶ Then the redeemer said, "I cannot redeem it for myself, lest I impair my own inheritance. Take my right of redemption yourself, for I cannot redeem it."*

⁷ Now this was the custom in former times in Israel concerning redeeming and exchanging: to confirm a transaction, the one drew off his sandal and gave it to the other, and this was the manner of attesting in Israel. [8] *So when the redeemer said to Boaz, "Buy it for yourself," he drew off his sandal.* [9] *Then Boaz said to the elders and all the people, "You are witnesses this day that I have bought from the hand of Naomi all that belonged to Elimelech and all that belonged to Chilion and to Mahlon.* [10] *Also Ruth the Moabite, the widow of Mahlon, I have bought to be my wife, to perpetuate the name of the dead in his inheritance, that the name of the dead may not be cut off from among his brothers and from the gate of his native place. You are witnesses this day."* [11] *Then all the people who were at the gate and the elders said, "We are witnesses. May the LORD make the woman, who is coming into your house, like Rachel and Leah, who together built up the house of Israel. May you act worthily in Ephrathah and be renowned in Bethlehem,* [12] *and may your house be like the house of Perez, whom Tamar bore to Judah, because of the offspring that the LORD will give you by this young woman."*

[13] *So Boaz took Ruth, and she became his wife. And he went in to her, and the LORD gave her conception, and she bore a son.* [14] *Then the women said to Naomi, "Blessed be the LORD, who has not left you this day without a redeemer, and may his name be renowned in Israel!* [15] *He*

shall be to you a restorer of life and a nourisher of your old age, for your daughter-in-law who loves you, who is more to you than seven sons, has given birth to him." ¹⁶ *Then Naomi took the child and laid him on her lap and became his nurse.* ¹⁷ *And the women of the neighborhood gave him a name, saying, "A son has been born to Naomi." They named him Obed. He was the father of Jesse, the father of David.*

¹⁸ *Now these are the generations of Perez: Perez fathered Hezron,* ¹⁹ *Hezron fathered Ram, Ram fathered Amminadab,* ²⁰ *Amminadab fathered Nahshon, Nahshon fathered Salmon,* ²¹ *Salmon fathered Boaz, Boaz fathered Obed,* ²² *Obed fathered Jesse, and Jesse fathered David.* (Ruth 4)

Life Is a Mountain Road

At one level, the message of the book of Ruth is that the life of the godly is not a straight line to glory, but they do get there. The life of the godly is not an interstate through Nebraska but a state road through the Blue Ridge Mountains of Tennessee. There are rockslides and precipices and dark mists and bears and slippery curves and hairpin turns that make you go backward in order to go forward. But all along this hazardous, twisted road that doesn't let you see very far ahead, there are frequent signs that say, "The best is yet to come."

Taken as a whole, the story of Ruth is one of those signs. It was written to give us encouragement and hope that all the perplexing turns in our lives are going somewhere good. They do not lead off a cliff. In all the setbacks of our lives as believers, God is plotting for our joy.

The Switchbacks on the Way Home

Taken in its parts, the book of Ruth is a series of setbacks—what we call switchbacks on the mountain road. You wonder how it will turn out. Will this strange road really lead home?

In chapter 1, Naomi and her husband and two sons are forced to leave their homeland in Judah on account of famine. Then Naomi's husband dies. Her sons marry Moabite women, and for ten years the women prove to be barren. Then her sons die, leaving two widows in the house of Naomi. Even though Ruth cleaves to Naomi, the chapter ends with Naomi's bitter complaint: "I went away full, and the LORD has brought me back empty . . . . The Almighty has dealt very bitterly with me."

In chapter 2, Naomi is filled with new hope because Boaz appears on the scene as a possible husband for

Ruth. But he doesn't propose to Ruth. He doesn't make any moves. At least that's the way it seems at first. So the chapter closes brimming with excited hope, but also with great suspense and uncertainty about how all this might work out.

In chapter 3, Naomi and Ruth make a risky move in the middle of the night. Ruth goes to Boaz on the threshing floor and says in effect, "I want you to spread your wings over me as my husband." But right when the tragedy of Ruth's widowhood seems to be resolved into a beautiful love story, a big mountain boulder rolls out onto the state road of Ruth's life. Another man, not Boaz, has a prior claim to marry Ruth. The impeccably honest Boaz will not proceed without giving this man his lawful opportunity. So chapter 3 ends in the suspense of another setback.

Life is not a straight line leading from one blessing to the next and then finally to heaven. Life is a winding and troubled road. Switchback after switchback. And the point of biblical stories like Joseph and Job and Esther and Ruth is to help us feel in our bones (not just know in our heads) that God is for us in all these strange turns. God is not just showing up after the trouble and cleaning it up. He is plotting the course and managing the troubles with far-reaching purposes for our good and for the glory of Jesus Christ.

The Threat of Ill-Timed Righteousness

After the midnight rendezvous in chapter 3, Boaz goes to the city gate where the official business was done. The nearer kinsman comes by, and Boaz lays the situation before him. Naomi is giving up what little property she has, and the duty of the nearer kinsman is to buy it so that the inheritance stays in the family. To our dismay, the kinsman says, "I will redeem it" (4:4).

We don't want him to redeem it. We want Boaz to redeem it. So again there seems to be a setback. And the irony of this setback is that it is being caused by righteousness. Boaz is doing the right thing. This other fellow is doing the right thing. Sometimes the Blue Ridge highway is all clogged up, not with boulders or bears, but with good workmen doing only their duty. Our frustrations are not only caused by sin but also by (seemingly!) ill-timed righteousness.

Just when we are about to say, "Oh no! Stop the story! Don't let this other fellow take Ruth!" Boaz says to the nearer kinsman, in my paraphrase of verse 5, "You know, don't you, that Naomi has a daughter-in-law? So when you play the part of the kinsman redeemer, you must also take her as your wife and raise up offspring in the name of her husband, Mahlon." Then, to our great relief, the kinsman says he can't do it (4:6). Perhaps he is married already. Whatever the reason, we are cheering in the background as Boaz gets through the bottleneck on the Blue Ridge highway and highballs it to the wedding feast with the beautiful young Ruth on his arm.

The Boulder of Barrenness

But there is another boulder in this happy road. Ruth is barren. Or at least she seems to be. Back in chapter 1, we were told that she had been married ten years to Mahlon, and there were no children (1:4). So even now the suspense is not over. But the cloud over the heads of Ruth and Boaz is big with mercy and breaks with blessing on their heads.

The jubilant friends of Boaz and Ruth pray for the newlyweds.

> May the LORD make the woman, who is coming into your house, like Rachel and Leah, who together built up the house of Israel. May you act worthily in Ephrathah and be renowned in Bethlehem, and may your house be like the house of Perez,

whom Tamar bore to Judah, because of the offspring
that the LORD will give you by this young woman.
(4:11–12)

They know that Rachel and Leah were alternately
barren and fruitful and that it was God who opened
and shut their wombs. "[God] opened [Leah's] womb,
but Rachel was barren" (Gen. 29:31). Then "Leah saw
that she had ceased bearing children" (Gen. 30:9). "God
remembered Rachel, and God listened to her and opened
her womb" (Gen. 30:22). These friends also knew that
Rachel and Leah were the great matriarchs of Israel.
They and their handmaids had given birth to the twelve
patriarchs of Israel.

Therefore, the prayer that Ruth be like Rachel and
Leah was a plea not only that God would open Ruth's
womb, but also that Ruth would take her place in the
great line of Israel leading to the Messiah. This was
the ultimate significance of their prayer that Boaz,
through his marriage to Ruth, would be "renowned in
Bethlehem." That is in fact where the greatest of all
Ruth's sons would be born. "So Boaz took Ruth, and
she became his wife. And he went in to her, and the
LORD gave her conception, and she bore a son" (Ruth
4:13).

Closing the Circle for Naomi

But now there is a surprising shift in chapter 4. Notice how the focus in verses 14–17 is not on Ruth at all, nor on Boaz. The focus is on Naomi and the child. Why?

The story began with Naomi's losses. It ends with Naomi's gain. It began with death and ends with birth. A son is born. Whose son is it? Of course, we would say, it is Ruth's son—Ruth's and Boaz's. But that is not what it says. It says, "A son has been born to Naomi" (4:17). Not only to Ruth but also to Naomi!

Why does it say that? To make crystal clear the complete reversal of Naomi's situation. She had said in Ruth 1:21, "I went away full, and the LORD has brought me back empty." But now she is full, and the Lord has given her a son through Ruth. God was at work in the darkest times to bring about this amazing turn of events. If we would trust God implicitly, like Ruth, we would find that all our complaints against God are unwarranted. Our providences may be bitter, but God is at work for our good—whether we can see it or not.

Is Glory Too Big a Word?

The book of Ruth was written to help us see the signposts of grace in our lives—the ones that are visible.

It also was written to help us trust God's grace when the clouds are so thick that we can't see the road, let alone the signs on the side. Again and again in this book, God is at work in the setbacks of Naomi. When she lost her husband and sons, God gave her Ruth. When she could think of no kinsman to raise up off-spring for the family, God gave her Boaz. When barren Ruth married Boaz, God gave the child. The life of the godly is not a straight line to glory, but God sees that they get there.

Maybe you think the word *glory* is a little overdone. After all it's just a child—a grandmother holding a little child after a long hard life of much heartache. But that is not the end of the story. The scope of this story is much greater than Naomi's life—or our lives.

In 1912, John Henry Jowett, then pastor of the Fifth Presbyterian Church in New York City, gave the Yale Lectures on Preaching. A passage in one of his lectures describes great preaching. It's relevant here because it gives us a vision of what the author of the book of Ruth was doing when he ended his story. A great preacher, Jowett says, is one who is able

> to look at the horizon rather than at an enclosed field,
> or a local landscape. He [has] a marvelous way of

connecting every subject with eternity past and with
eternity to come. . . . It is as though you were looking
at a bit of carved wood in a Swiss village window,
and you lifted your eyes and saw the forest where the
wood was nourished, and, higher still, the everlasting
snows! Yes, that was Binney's way, Dale's way, the
way of Bushnell, and Newman, and Spurgeon—they
were always willing to stop at the village window,
but they always linked the streets with the heights,
and sent your souls a-roaming over the eternal hills
of God.[1]

If this story of Ruth just ended in a little Judean village
with an old grandmother hugging a new grandson, *glory*
would be too big a word. But the author doesn't leave it
there. He lifts his eyes to the forests and to the mountain
snows of redemptive history.

Preparing the Lineage of the Greatest King

In 4:17, we read very simply that this child named Obed
was the father of Jesse, and Jesse was the father of
David. Suddenly we realize that all along something far
greater has been in the offing than we could imagine.

[1]John Henry Jowett, *The Preacher: His Life and Work* (New York: Harper,
1912), 95.

God was not only plotting for the temporal blessing of a few Jews in Bethlehem. He was preparing for the coming of the greatest king that Israel would have, David.

And the name of David carries with it the hope of the Messiah, the new age, peace, righteousness, freedom from pain and crying and grief and guilt. This simple little story opens out like a stream into an ocean of hope.

From David to Jesus

Jesus is the one who made this connection for us between David and himself. He asked the Pharisees,

> "What do you think about the Christ? Whose son is he?" They said to him, "The son of David." He said to them, "How is it then that David, in the Spirit, calls him Lord, saying, 'The Lord said to my Lord, Sit at my right hand, until I put your enemies under your feet'? If then David calls him Lord, how is he his son?" And no one was able to answer him a word, nor from that day did anyone dare to ask him any more questions. (Matt. 22:41–46)

The point of what Jesus said was that he himself is the son of David and that he is far more than merely a human son of David. David calls him *Lord*. So how is he his son? Jesus wants us to see that already in the Old

Testament (Ps. 110:1) we learn that the coming of the Messiah, as the son of David, would be vastly more than the Pharisees thought. He would be son of David and *Lord* of David.

Who Is the Redeemer?

Did the writer of the book of Ruth see the greatness of the future implied in the reference to David? It may be that the writer saw even more. Listen to these amazing words:

> Then the women said to Naomi, "Blessed be the LORD, who has not left you this day without a redeemer, and may his name be renowned in Israel! He shall be to you a restorer of life and a nourisher of your old age, for your daughter-in-law who loves you, who is more to you than seven sons, has given birth to him." (Ruth 4:14–15)

What is amazing here is that the "redeemer" is the baby. At first, we might think that the word *redeemer* here (4:14) would refer to Boaz (3:9, 12), since he is the one who "redeemed" the property and the name of Naomi's husband. But that is not the natural way to understand verses 14–15. The *he* at the beginning of verse 15 refers to the "redeemer" in verse 14, and it does not refer to Boaz. "He shall be to you a restorer of life and a nourisher of your old age." That is what the child will do, not Boaz.

Renowned and Redeeming through Jesus Christ

So why is this child called a *redeemer*? At one level, he simply redeems Naomi from hopelessness in her old age. He refreshes her and gives life to her despairing heart. But there is another level of meaning. This child will be the grandfather of David (4:22) who receives the promise that his offspring will rule over an eternal kingdom (2 Sam. 7:13), and the name of this child will be "renowned in Israel" (Ruth 4:14). These two (the renown and the connection with David) are probably linked. The renown of this child will not be mainly in himself; it will come through his offspring, David—and through David's offspring, the Messiah.

That suggests that the child's redeemer role also is not simply in himself, but through his offspring. He will redeem by bringing forth a redeemer. From our standpoint with fuller biblical revelation, we can see this, first, in the great deliverances of David and then, beyond him, in the greatest redemption of all—the redemption through David's son, Jesus Christ. "Christ redeemed us from the curse of the law by becoming a curse for us" (Gal. 3:13). He "gave himself for us to redeem us from all lawlessness" (Titus 2:14). "Blessed be the Lord God of Israel, for he has visited and redeemed his people" (Luke 1:68).

Looking to the Farthest Meaning

The story of Ruth, at one level, is about God's sweet and bitter providences. He governs the famine, and the marriage of Naomi's sons to foreign women, and the death of her sons, and the faithfulness of Ruth, and the availability and nobility of Boaz, and the birth of a child to preserve the line of Elimelech. The story shows that God is at work in the darkest of times for the good of his people. The life of believers is not a straight path to glory, but they do get there.

But at another level, the story is about something much larger than one family and their sorrows and joys. It is about God's plan to glorify his grace in the Son of David, the Messiah, the Redeemer, Jesus Christ. Ruth and Naomi and Boaz are caught up in something of eternal significance. *Glory* is not too big a word for the destinies implicit in this story.

Seeing Ourselves in Undeserving Ruth

The application of this glory to us may be felt most personally when we focus on Ruth herself. How are we included? All the calamities of this story seem to be designed to get a Moabitess into the genealogy of Jesus. Ruth is one of the four women mentioned in Matthew's genealogy (Matt. 1:5). God pursued her. He turned the world upside down, you might say, to include Ruth in the lineage of his Son.

Surely this is significant for us. Does it not mean that God's blessings are free and undeserved? Ruth was an idolatrous Moabitess before God pursued her (Ruth 1:15). She did not merit this pursuit. It was free. That is the way God pursues you and me. "You did not choose me, but I chose you" (John 15:16).

Making Christ a Moabite

Not only that, but God moved the world in order to include a foreigner in the lineage of the Messiah. Ruth was not a Jew. Is not God showing us that his heart is for the nations—all the nations? The glory of Christ is that he comes from the nations and dies for the nations. His blood was shed for the nations, and the nations' blood ran in his veins. The Jewish high priest prophesied better than he knew in John 11:51–52 "that Jesus would die for the nation, and not for the nation only, but also to gather into one the children of God who are scattered abroad." "You were slain, and by your blood you ransomed people for God from every tribe and language and people and nation" (Rev. 5:9).

The redeeming work of Christ is free and undeserved. It is intended for every ethnic group on the planet. All ethnocentric and racist impulses are crucified in Christ. That too is what the story of Ruth is about.

Planning Christ through Great Wickedness

There is one more implication of this story that I want to draw out. It is not obvious until it is pointed out. Then it is striking. The writer of this story aims to show that God was at work in the time of the judges (Ruth 1:1) to prepare the way for David the king (4:22). The first and last verses of the book make this plain.

But during the time of the judges, there were no kings. In fact, during the time of the judges, it was sin to demand a king. Nevertheless, near the end of this period, the people asked for a king.

> Then all the elders of Israel gathered together and came to Samuel at Ramah and said to him, "Behold,

you are old and your sons do not walk in your ways. Now appoint for us a king to judge us like all the nations." But the thing displeased Samuel when they said, "Give us a king to judge us." And Samuel prayed to the LORD. And the LORD said to Samuel, "Obey the voice of the people in all that they say to you, for they have not rejected you, but they have rejected me from being king over them." (1 Sam. 8:4–7)

Asking for a king meant that they were rejecting God as their king. This, Samuel says, was a great wickedness: "Your wickedness is great, which you have done in the sight of the LORD, in asking for yourselves a king" (1 Sam. 12:17).

Nevertheless, the book of Ruth is written with a clear sense of joy that Ruth and Naomi and Boaz are the forebears of the king of Israel. So in the same period when it was a "great wickedness" to ask for a king, God was preparing to give the people a king. We are meant to conclude that, without approving of sin, God governs the sinful acts of men for his own good and wise purposes. He was planning that Israel would have a king, though it was sin for the people to demand one. In fact, it was precisely through this sin that the kingly line was started, from which, in the end, the King of kings would come.

"We have added to all our sins this evil, to ask for ourselves a king." And Samuel said to the people, "Do not be afraid; you have done all this evil. Yet do not turn aside from following the LORD, but serve the LORD with all your heart. . . . For the LORD will not forsake his people, for his great name's sake." (1 Sam. 12:19–20, 22)

God had mercy on the people and made their sinful act serve his eternal purposes—that there would be a kingly line and that his Son would be the glorious climax of that line.[2]

No Cross without Sovereignty over Sin

This amazing fact brings us to the cross of Christ in more ways than one. We ask: *Can it really be that God governs the sinful acts of men to make them serve his wise purposes without himself being a sinner?* Yes, he can. If he cannot, then there is no Christian gospel. The gospel is the good news that Christ died for our sins. "Now I would remind you, brothers, of the gospel . . . that Christ died for our sins in accordance with the Scriptures, that he was buried, that he was raised

[2]This is one of many instances in the Bible where God's sovereignty over sin is made to serve the glory of Christ. That is the main point of my book *Spectacular Sins: And Their Global Purpose for the Glory of Christ* (Wheaton, IL: Crossway Books, 2008).

on the third day in accordance with the Scriptures" (1 Cor. 15:1–4).

Notice the repeated phrase "in accordance with the Scriptures." That means that God planned it. God planned that Christ would die. There would be no gospel without the death of Christ. All the deeds that brought him to the cross were planned. This is explicit in the early church's prayer of praise in Acts 4:27–28:

> Truly in this city there were gathered together against your holy servant Jesus, whom you anointed, both Herod and Pontius Pilate, along with the Gentiles and the peoples of Israel, to do whatever your hand and your plan had predestined to take place.

This means that what Herod, Pilate, the soldiers, and the mobs did to Jesus was planned by God. And all those acts against Jesus were sin.

God does not sin. He is holy (Isa. 6:3). He "is light, and in him is no darkness at all" (1 John 1:5). He is "the Father of lights" from whom comes "every good gift and every perfect gift" (James 1:17). But he clearly ordained that the murder of his Son happen. In other words, when we see God's sovereignty at work in the book of Ruth preparing the line of a king, even though asking for that king was sin, we are seeing the kind of divine work that is necessary for the redemption of the world. There could be no crucifixion if there were no crucifiers.

The Cross: God's Loving Plan

Perhaps someone may think that this heady theology about God's ruling over sin without being sinful himself is too high to be practically helpful. Joni Eareckson Tada and her coauthor Steve Estes have found it otherwise.

Joni has been almost completely paralyzed from the neck down from a diving accident when she was seventeen years old. During a bleak period of doubt and anger, a friend introduced her to Steve Estes. They began to study the Bible together. "She came to the classically Reformed belief that her injury was an expression of God's love. To put it simply, Scripture taught Tada that her soul was infinitely more important than her body."[3]

She explains,

> I was heading down a path of self-destruction [before my accident]. . . . I was checking out a birth-control clinic to get some pills, because I knew I'd be sleeping with my boyfriend in college. Somewhere

[3]Tim Stafford, "A Heaven-Made Activist," *Christianity Today*, Vol. 48, No. 1 (January 2004): 49.

in that mess of emotions and regrets and falterings and failings, while making a sham of my Christian faith, somewhere in that desperation I said, "God, rescue me." And he did. I believe my accident was a direct answer.

Some people might want to say indirect, but I lean toward the old adage that God draws straight lines with crooked sticks.[4]

In other words, when God ordains something crooked, he himself is not doing anything crooked. When told that many people would say, "How dare you say God did that?" she recalls that she had the same question for Steve Estes. "How in the world can you say this accident was God's will?" Here's where God's sovereignty over the cross of Christ becomes so relevant.

She recalls that Steve answered,

Let me answer that question by asking you a question. Do you believe that when Jesus died on the cross, that was God's will? . . .

Well, think about it for a minute, because Jesus was handed over for 30 pieces of silver, drunken soldiers pulled his beard out, then beat him mercilessly in that back room. The mob screamed, "Crucify him."

[4]Ibid.

How can that be God's will? Torture, injustice, murder, treason. How could any of that be God's will?[5]

Joni remembers, "He had me. Because I knew that God the Father's plan was for his Son to go to the cross."[6] These insights led Joni to the deep and unshakable conviction that the pains of life are not exceptions to God's love for his children. They are expressions of his love. "There are more important things than walking," she says.

> Maybe death is supposed to be hard. Maybe it's supposed to be a taste of hell. . . . Oh, thank you, thank you for this wheelchair! By tasting hell in this life, I've been driven to think seriously about what faces me in the next. This paralysis is my greatest mercy.[7]

A vision of God as absolutely supreme over all the evil of the world—natural and moral—has set Joni Eareckson Tada free to love others. Tim Stafford, who interviewed Joni for an article in *Christianity Today*, said, "Heaven has pulled her out of herself, and into the lives of other sufferers. Heaven has made Tada an activist."[8]

[5]Ibid., 50.
[6]Ibid.
[7]Ibid.
[8]Ibid.

God's sovereignty over sin, even the world's worst sin—murdering the Son of God—was not too high to help Joni Eareckson Tada. And it is not too high to help you.

Ruth against Rampant Trifling

The implications of the story of Ruth are breathtaking. They are bigger than the world and bigger than our minds. Like all Scripture, this story is inexhaustible. We have perhaps scratched the surface.

One of the great diseases of our day is trifling. The things with which most people spend most of their time are trivial. And what makes this a disease is that we were meant to live for magnificent causes. None of us is really content with the trivial pursuits of the world. Our souls will not be satisfied with trifles. Why is there a whole section of the newspaper devoted to sports and almost nothing devoted to the greatest story in the universe—the growth and spread of the church of Jesus Christ? It is madness that insignificant games should occupy such a central role in our culture compared to the work of God in Christ.

It is one of many signs that we are enslaved to trivialities. We live in the Swiss village but stare at the wooden figurines in the window rather than lifting our eyes to the "everlasting snows." We live in a perpetual and hopeless struggle to satisfy our longings on trifles. So our souls shrivel. Our lives become trivial. And our capacity for magnificent causes and great worship dies.

Something Greater Than Ourselves

The book of Ruth wants to teach us that God's purpose for his people is to connect us to something far greater than ourselves. God wants us to know that when we follow him, our lives always mean more than we think they do. Naomi had no idea in the land of Moab that God was making her the ancestor of the Messiah. For the Christian there is always a connection between the ordinary events of life and the stupendous work of God in history.

Everything we do in obedience to God, no matter how small, is significant. It is part of a cosmic mosaic that God is painting to display the greatness of his power and wisdom to the world and to the principalities and powers in the heavenly places (Eph. 3:10). A deep satisfaction of the Christian life is that we are not given over to trifles. Serving a widowed mother-in-law, gleaning in a field, falling in love, having a baby—for the Christian these things are all connected to eternity. They are part of something so much bigger than they seem.

The Best Is Yet to Come—Glory

So the word *glory* is not too strong for where this book leads us. The life of the godly is not a straight line to glory, but they do get there—God sees to it. There is a hope for us beyond the cute baby and the happy grandmother. The story points forward to David. David points forward to Jesus. And Jesus points forward to the resurrection of our mortal bodies (Rom. 8:23) when "death shall be no more, neither shall there be mourning, nor crying, nor pain anymore, for the former things have passed away" (Rev. 21:4).

The best is yet to come. That is the unshakable truth about the life of the woman and the man who follow Christ in the obedience that flows from faith. I say it to the young who are strong and hopeful, and I say it to the old, for whom the outer nature is quickly wasting away. The best is yet to come. And God is at work in the darkest of your times to get you there.

"Sweetie-Pie"

This pledge God has made to his people is unbreakable. No famine or death can break it. I saw it in a parable. I was visiting some of our elderly people in a nursing home. I got on the elevator with a woman in a wheelchair who was old, misshapen, and confused. Her head wobbled meaninglessly, and she uttered senseless sounds. Her mouth hung open. Then I noticed that a well-dressed man, perhaps in his mid-sixties, was pushing her chair. I wondered who he was. Then as we all got off the elevator, I heard him say, "Watch your feet, Sweetie-pie."

Sweetie-pie. As I walked to the car, I thought . . . if a marriage covenant between a man and a woman produces that kind of fidelity and commitment and affection under those circumstances, then surely under the great and merciful terms of the New Covenant, sealed with the blood of his Son (Luke 22:20), God has no difficulty calling you and me (sinful and sick as we are) sweet names. And if he does, there is no truth more unshakable in all the world than this: for them and for us, the best is yet to come. God is at work in the darkest times—for our good and Christ's glory. He will see to it that the glory of his Son fills the earth and that in him we find everlasting joy.

FINAL APPEALS

WE END WHERE WE BEGAN. In the Introduction, I mentioned seven reasons why I thought you might want to read this book. In closing, I will take those seven reasons and turn them into seven appeals. If I have understood the story of Ruth correctly, these are not merely my appeals, but also God's. I give them in the spirit of Romans 12:1—because God has been merciful to us: "I appeal to you . . . by the mercies of God." Yes, by his mercies and for his glory.

1. Study the Scriptures

In September 1966, I was lying sick with mononucleosis in the health center at Wheaton College. Harold John Ockenga was preaching in chapel across campus. I listened on WETN radio. I was a junior in premed, but that preaching changed everything.

Inside of me there awakened a desire that has never died—a desire to know and study the Bible. Before I left the health center, I had resolved to attend seminary. I didn't know my calling then. All I knew was that there was in me a passion to understand Scripture—and to help others love it and live it.

That was forty-four years ago. My hunger has never changed. I am writing this simply to encourage you to do the same. Not that everyone should go to seminary or become a full-time student of the Bible. But everyone should make a lifelong habit of growing in the knowledge and love of God's Word.

The Scriptures are "true and righteous altogether. More to be desired are they than gold, even much fine gold; sweeter also than honey and drippings of the honeycomb. Moreover, by them is your servant warned; in keeping them there is great reward" (Ps. 19:9–11).

Compared to whatever else you might read—and we must read other things—only the Scriptures give life. "Lord, to whom shall we go? You have the words of eternal life" (John 6:68). Only the Scriptures can defeat the supernatural power of evil. "The word of God abides in you, and you have overcome the evil one" (1 John 2:14). Only the Scriptures are infallible and lead you unfailingly in the truth. "Scripture cannot be broken" (John 10:35). Only the Word of God can cause new birth. "You have been born again . . . through the living and abiding word of God" (1 Pet. 1:23–25). Only the Word of God can make us holy. "Sanctify them in the truth; your word is truth" (John 17:17). Only the Scriptures awaken lasting spiritual joy. "These things I have spoken to you, that my joy may be in you, and that your joy may be full" (John 15:11).

I owe my life to the Word of God. I owe my faith and hope and preaching and counseling and writing and marriage and friendships and perseverance to the Word of God. I shudder at the thought of life without the Bible. Here is where I meet Jesus. Here is where I fellowship with him and consult with him and learn from him and get corrected by him and comforted by him. Joyful fellowship with Jesus is inconceivable apart from his living Word and presence through the Bible.

I want everyone to know and trust and love and follow Jesus Christ. This is possible only through the biblical Word. So I pray that our trek together through the story of Ruth will stir you up to go on. There are discoveries waiting for you that will change your life. There is more of God to be known and more of Christ to be seen than you ever thought possible. There is a strength of soul, and a clarity of faith, and a firmness of hope, and a height of joy, and a depth of wisdom, and a genuineness of love, and a quiet peace, and a humble boldness that only comes from rich seasons of meditation on the Word of God.

May the Lord awaken in you an insatiable hunger for his Word. "'Feed your belly with this scroll that I give you and fill your stomach with it.' Then I ate it, and it was in my mouth as sweet as honey" (Ezek. 3:3).

2. Pursue Sexual Purity

One of the things Scripture does is entice us to a deeper, stronger, more beautiful view of human sexuality. To be sure, what the world offers is "powerful," but only in the visceral way. It's powerful the way appetite is powerful. But humans are created in God's image. We are more than a collection of appetites.

Ruth is a story of another kind of sexual power—like a river running deep between the high banks of righteousness. Without banks, a river overflows everywhere and creates havoc. It also gets muddy and shallow. That's what happens to sex without the restraints of God.

But when this river runs between the banks of biblical truth, it runs deep, and it runs pure. Those who give themselves away outside marriage forfeit a depth of pleasure that only those know who wait for the Lord.

Experiencing sexual purity by the power of God's Spirit and the truth of God's word carries a reward that those outside cannot feel.

It has to do with seeing God. "Blessed are the pure in heart, for they shall see God" (Matt. 5:8). George Whitefield said, "He who is most pure in heart, shall hereafter enjoy the clearest vision of God."[1] Yes. But not just in the hereafter. Our sight of God in the present is clouded by all impurity.

This is the greatest argument for a life free from fornication and adultery and pornography and lustful imaginations. It lets you see more of God. This is what we were made for. Moses cried, "Show me your glory" (Ex. 33:18). Jesus prayed for us, "Father, I desire that they also, whom you have given me, may be with me where I am, to see my glory" (John 17:24).

It is a great tragedy—a great loss—when a person chooses sexual license over seeing God. It is like Einstein choosing to be a janitor, or Billy Graham choosing to be a newscaster, or Michael Jordan choosing to play baseball. It's not what we are made for. We were made to see God, know God, admire God, enjoy God. Stay sexually pure, and pursue the pleasures that never fail.

[1] George Whitefield, "Christ, the Believer's Wisdom, Righteousness, Sanctification and Redemption," in *Select Sermons of George Whitefield* (Edinburgh: The Banner of Truth Trust, 1985), 114.

3. Pursue Mature Manhood and Womanhood

The egalitarian impulses of the last thirty years have not made us better men and women. In fact, they have confused millions. What average man or woman today could answer a little boy's question, *Daddy, what does it mean to grow up and be a man and not a woman?* Or a little girl's question, *Mommy, what does it mean to grow up and be a woman and not a man?*

Who could answer these questions without diminishing manhood and womanhood into mere biological mechanisms? Who could articulate the profound meanings of manhood and womanhood woven differently into a common personhood created differently and equally in the image of God? James Dobson puts it like this: "At the heart . . . is the issue of *what is a man?* If you try to reduce that issue to just: *what is a caring person*, you make a good point but miss a crucial created element called manhood that *is* relevant."[2] Not asking the question about the essence of male and female personhood confuses everyone, especially the children.

And this confusion hurts people. It is not a small thing. Its effects are vast. I agree with Dobson when he says, "Feminist resistance to making manhood and

[2]*Focus on the Family*, May 1993, Vol. 17, No. 5, 7. Final italics original.

womanhood significant in behavior and role determination is partner to some of the most painful social and spiritual issues of our day."[3]

When manhood and womanhood are confused at home, the consequences are deeper than may show up in a generation. There are dynamics in the home that direct the sexual preferences of the children and shape their concept of manhood and womanhood. Especially crucial in the matter of sexual preference is a father's firm and loving affirmation of a son's masculinity and a daughter's femininity.[4] The father must be a man. But how can this kind of manly affirmation be cultivated in an atmosphere where role differences between masculinity and femininity are constantly denied or diminished for the sake of gender-leveling and sex-blindness?

What we all need is solid teaching from the Bible about the differences God intends between men and women.[5] But we also need stories. Great stories. We need to see manhood and womanhood in action—in real life and fiction and history. The story of Ruth and Boaz is the

[3]Ibid.
[4]Gerald P. Regier, "The Not-So-Disposable Family," *Pastoral Renewal*, Vol. 13, No. 1 (July-August 1988): 20.
[5]I have tried to think this through in a small way in *What's the Difference? Manhood and Womanhood Defined According to the Bible* (Wheaton, IL: Crossway, 2009). See also John Piper and Wayne Grudem, eds., *Recovering Biblical Manhood and Womanhood* (Wheaton, IL: Crossway, 2006), and Wayne Grudem, *Evangelical Feminism and Biblical Truth* (Wheaton, IL: Crossway, 2013). See also www.cbmw.org.

kind of story that can awaken and feed the masculine and feminine soul in ways that we cannot articulate.

I encourage you to be like a dolphin in the sea of our egalitarian, gender-leveling culture. Don't be like a jellyfish. The ocean of secularism that we swim in (including much of the church) drifts toward minimizing serious differences between manhood and womanhood. The culture swings back and forth as to whether women are mainly sex objects or senior vice presidents, or whether they are both—in the image of pistol-whipping, male-dominating beauties. But rarely does it ponder the biblical vision that men are called to humbly lead and protect and provide, and women are called to come in alongside with their unique gifts and strengths and help the men carry through the vision.

I pray that you will be stirred up by Ruth and Boaz to pursue mature manhood and womanhood. More is at stake than we know. God has made marriage the showcase of his covenant love where the husband models Christ, and the wife models the church (Eph. 5:21–33). And God calls single people to bless this vision and to cultivate an expression of leadership and support appropriate to their different relationships.[6]

[6]For more on this vision of marriage, see John Piper, *This Momentary Marriage: A Parable of Permanence* (Wheaton, IL: Crossway, 2009).

4. Embrace Ethnic Diversity

If you read the book of Ruth backward—knowing the resolution before you know how we get there—it is astonishing that the story is built precisely to include a Moabite woman in the lineage of David and the Messiah. This intentionality is underlined in Matthew 1:5 where Ruth is one of the four women mentioned in the genealogy of Jesus.

In fact, it seems that Matthew was going out of his way to include unlikely women in his genealogy: Tamar who bore Perez through adultery with her father-in-law (Matt. 1:3), Rahab the Canaanite prostitute (Matt. 1:5), and Bathsheba, the wife of a Hittite who committed adultery with King David and bore Solomon (Matt. 1:6). I say *unlikely* both because of ethnic and moral reasons.

Ruth was not an Israelite. This meant she was ethnically an outsider to the covenant and to the customs and laws of Israel. Israelites were not supposed to marry women of other nations (Ezra 10:11). During the same period of the judges when the story of Ruth took place (Ruth 1:1), Samson's parents said to him, "Is there not a woman among the daughters of your relatives, or among all our people, that you must go to take a wife from the uncircumcised Philistines?" (Judg. 14:3).

What God was doing in his far-seeing providence was planting the dynamite that would explode the fortresses of ethnocentrism and racism. As the history of his people progressed, God would make it clearer and clearer that the real issue in intermarriage was not race but faith. Paul would eventually say that a follower of Christ should marry "only in the Lord" (1 Cor. 7:39).

I have spelled out a biblical position on ·interracial marriage in a sermon titled "Racial Harmony and Interracial Marriage."[7] Here I simply want to celebrate God's aim to call a people from all the ethnic groups of the world. The story of Ruth tells us that Moabite blood flowed in the veins of the Son of God. This blood was then shed for the salvation of Moabites—and every other people group. "You were slain, and by your blood you ransomed people for God from every tribe and language and people and nation" (Rev. 5:9).

The global ground where we stand is shifting under our feet. Peoples are moving as never before. For example, the Twin Cities of Minneapolis and St. Paul

---

[7]Available online at http://www.desiringgod.org. See also chapter 15 in John Piper, *Bloodlines: Race, Cross, and the Christian* (Wheaton, IL: Crossway, 2011).

where I live is presently home to the largest Somali and Hmong populations in the United States, as well as the largest Chinese student population. Phillips Neighborhood, where our house is located, is one of the most diverse neighborhoods in the country, with more than a hundred different languages. Nearby Nicollet Avenue's "Eat Street" has seventy-five ethnic restaurants in a six-block area. One of our suburbs, Maple Grove, is home to the largest Hindu temple in North America. The same kinds of shifting are happening all over the world.

None of this is any more accidental than Naomi's stay in Moab. God was drawing Ruth to himself, and today he is drawing thousands of ethnic peoples to himself. God loves to magnify the power of his Son to call people from every group. And he loves to magnify the beauty of his Son to hold the allegiance of hearts in every kind of culture.

Don't let the shifting of peoples and cultures that you see threaten your faith. Don't cleave to the way things are as if your citizenship is merely on earth. "Our citizenship is in heaven, and from it we await a Savior, the Lord Jesus Christ" (Phil. 3:20). Whatever country we live in, we are "sojourners and exiles" (1 Pet. 2:11). A follower of Christ in any ethnic group is a closer relative to us than any blood relative who rejects our Savior. "Whoever does the will of God, he is my brother and sister and mother" (Mark 3:35).

5. Trust the Sovereignty of God

I think God has revealed his sovereignty to us so that we will feel a suitable reverence at his power and a strong confidence that we are loved. It is fitting that we tremble at the majesty of God's power. "This is the one to whom I will look: he who is humble and contrite in spirit and *trembles at my word*" (Isa. 66:2). "When I saw him, I fell at his feet as though dead" (Rev. 1:17).

It is also fitting that those who are in Christ never fear any condemnation (Rom. 8:1), nor ever dream that God has turned against them. "If God is for us, who can be against us? He who did not spare his own Son but gave him up for us all, how will he not also with him graciously give us all things?" (Rom. 8:31–32). When Christ absorbs the wrath of God that we deserved, God never aims at our destruction but only at our holy, eternal happiness.

The painful things that come into our lives are not described by God as accidental or as out of his control. This would be no comfort. That God cannot stop a germ or a car or a bullet or a demon is not good news; it is not the news of the Bible. God can. And ten thousand times he does. But when he doesn't, he has his reasons. And in Christ Jesus they are all loving. We are taught this sovereignty so that we will drink it in till it saturates our bones. He is getting us ready to suffer without feeling unloved.

So when suffering comes, God's children are meant to experience it as God's fatherly discipline. It does not speak well of our faith if we doubt his love or if we become angry at God when he ordains pain in our lives. The story of Ruth (along with Joseph and Job and Esther and others) is in the Bible to prepare us for bitter providences by showing us again and again that God is doing a thousand things that we do not know. And they are meant for our good.

> "My son, do not regard lightly the discipline of the Lord, nor be weary when reproved by him. For the Lord disciplines the one he loves, and chastises every son whom he receives." It is for discipline that you have to endure. God is treating you as sons. . . . For the moment all discipline seems painful rather than pleasant, but later it yields the peaceful fruit of righteousness to those who have been trained by it. (Heb. 12:5–8, 11)

This is how the children of God should experience the providence of God. We have often used the word *providence* in this book. Here is a beautiful description of it from the four-hundred-year-old Heidelberg Catechism:

> *Question 27:* What do you mean by the providence of God?
>
> *Answer:* The almighty and everywhere present power of God; whereby, as it were by his hand, he upholds and governs heaven, earth, and all creatures; so that herbs and grass, rain and drought, fruitful and barren years, meat and drink, health and sickness, riches and poverty, yea, and all things come, not by chance, but by his fatherly hand.

What I have tried to do in this book is draw out the personal and precious fact that this truth is comforting. Yes, it is painful. To know that our Father in heaven has ordained our pain is not a comfortable truth, but it is comforting. That our pain has a loving and wise and all-powerful purpose behind it is better than any other view—weak God, cruel God, bumbling God, no God. To know that in his hands "this light momentary affliction is preparing for us an eternal weight of glory beyond all comparison" (2 Cor. 4:17) is profoundly reassuring. And yes, "light" and "momentary" meant, in Paul's case, a *lifetime* of suffering. The excruciating[8] "lightness" of his suffering was light compared to the *weight* of glory. And the interminable "momentariness" of his suffering was momentary compared to the *eternality* of the glory.

My point is that there is a great advantage in knowing that God is sovereign over the pain and pleasure of our lives. The Heidelberg Catechism asks what this is and gives the answer:

> *Question 28:* What advantage is it to us to know that God has created, and by his providence does still uphold all things?
>
> *Answer:* That we may be patient in adversity; thankful in prosperity; and that in all things, which may hereafter befall us, we place our firm trust in our faithful God and Father, that nothing shall separate us from his love; since all creatures are so in his hand, that without his will they cannot so much as move.

---

[8]Paul lists some of his pains: ". . . far more imprisonments, with countless beatings, and often near death. Five times I received at the hands of the Jews the forty lashes less one. Three times I was beaten with rods. Once I was stoned. Three times I was shipwrecked; a night and a day I was adrift at sea; on frequent journeys, in danger from rivers, danger from robbers, danger from my own people, danger from Gentiles, danger in the city, danger in the wilderness, danger at sea, danger from false brothers; in toil and hardship, through many a sleepless night, in hunger and thirst, often without food, in cold and exposure. And, apart from other things, there is the daily pressure on me of my anxiety for all the churches. Who is weak, and I am not weak? Who is made to fall, and I am not indignant?" (2 Cor. 11:23–29).

If we can keep our eyes on the cross of Christ, where God infallibly certified his love for us with no change possible (Rom. 5:8; 1 John 3:16), then the pain he ordains for us will not undermine our sense of being loved. Instead, we will put our hands on our mouths and bow before his all-loving, all-ruling providence. We will trust him to only do us good— whether it feels good or not at the moment. And we will wait for the day when all will be repaid and made plain.

> *O Joy that seekest me through pain,*
> *I cannot close my heart to thee;*
> *I trace the rainbow through the rain,*
> *And feel the promise is not vain,*
> *That morn shall tearless be.*[9]

Even on this side of the tearless morning, there are often revelations of the glory of Christ in suffering that outstrip any visions that come on bright days. O how many suffering saints have found this to be so:

> *I learned He never gives a thorn without this*
> *   added grace,*
> *He takes the thorn to pin aside the veil which hides*
> *   His face.*[10]

[9]George Matheson, "O Love That Wilt Not Let Me Go," 1882.
[10]Martha Snell Nicholson, "The Thorn," in *The Glory Forever* (Chicago, IL: Moody Press, 1949), 17.

6. Take the Risks of Love

Ruth took the risks of love—leaving her homeland, promising never to return, working faithfully for her mother-in-law through the heat of the day, going to Boaz in the middle of the night—because she lived under the "wings [of God]" (Ruth 2:12). The sovereign goodness of God is revealed to us not only for our comfort, but also to free us from the fear and selfishness that quashes the radical risks of love.

Love is what faith looks like when we trust the sovereign promises of God secured by the blood of Christ. "In Christ Jesus neither circumcision nor uncircumcision counts for anything, but only *faith working through love*" (Gal. 5:6). Faith in God's sovereign love for us empowers works of love. Love displays the reality of faith in God's promises.

Therefore, Paul says that "the aim of our charge is love" (1 Tim. 1:5). That's what the author of the book of Ruth would have said too. The aim is not just to entertain us with an interesting story, not just to clarify our theology. The aim is that these clarified convictions and this inspiring story would empower us for radical, risk-taking works of love. These are the lights of the world that cause people to glorify God (Matt. 5:16).

Just before Jesus performed the greatest work of

love that ever was, he strengthened his heart with the joy that was set before him. This joy was secured by the sovereignty shared by his Father and himself. "No one takes it from me, but I lay it down of my own accord. I have authority to lay it down, and I have authority to take it up again. This charge I have received from my Father" (John 10:18). He was upheld with the hope of absolutely certain future joy: "For the joy that was set before him [he] endured the cross" (Heb. 12:2).

There is no safer place in all the universe than under the wings of the sovereign, all-wise, all-loving God. But the shadow of these wings may take us to dangerous places in the cause of love. You may be martyred in the shadow of the Almighty. But you will not have wasted your life when you die in the cause of love. As the martyr Jim Elliot famously said, "He is no fool who gives what he cannot keep to gain that which he cannot lose."[11]

7. Live and Sing to the Glory of Christ

What is implied at the end of Ruth—which looks forward to David and the messianic line of David—and what is

[11]Elisabeth Elliot, *Shadow of the Almighty: The Life and Testament of Jim Elliot* (New York: Harper & Brothers, 1958), 19.

clear from the eternal perspective of Scripture is that all of human history is for the glory of Jesus Christ. "All things were created through him and *for him*" (Col. 1:16).

From eternity to eternity, Christ is in view as the focus of all worship and allegiance. Before creation, God planned our redemption. And the focus of it from eternity past was Christ: "He chose us *in him* before the foundation of the world" (Eph. 1:4). Before creation God planned the death of his Son. He prepared a book of the redeemed "before the foundation of the world" and gave the book a name: "the book of life of the Lamb who was slain" (Rev. 13:8).

And at the other end of eternity, we will sing to the Lamb at the center of all our worship. There will be no competition between God the Father and God the Son for our worship, because the Lamb is "in the midst" of the throne of God (Rev. 7:17). The throne of the universe is "the throne of God and of the Lamb" (Rev. 22:1, 3). And there is no hesitation to say, "Salvation belongs to our God who sits on the throne, and to the Lamb!" (Rev. 7:10). Every creature will cry, "To him who sits on the throne and to the Lamb be blessing and honor and glory and might forever and ever!" (Rev. 5:13).

When the Father becomes "all in all" (1 Cor. 15:28), the Son, Jesus Christ, the Lamb who was slain, will not be less than supremely worshiped with the Father. He will have his praise for his unique work.

> Then I looked, and I heard around the throne and the living creatures and the elders the voice of many angels, numbering myriads of myriads and thousands of thousands, saying with a loud voice,
>
> *"Worthy is the Lamb who was slain,*
> *to receive power and wealth and wisdom and might*
> *and honor and glory and blessing!"*
>
> And I heard every creature in heaven and on earth and under the earth and in the sea, and all that is in them, saying,
>
> *"To him who sits on the throne and to the Lamb be*
> *blessing and honor and glory and might forever*
> *and ever!"*
>
> And the four living creatures said, "Amen!" and the elders fell down and worshiped. (Rev. 5:11–14)

Ruth and Boaz and Naomi are there glorifying Christ. They know now how the story ends. And so do we—even before we get there. Therefore, make a good beginning in this world: live and sing to the glory of Christ.

ACKNOWLEDGMENTS

BETHLEHEM BAPTIST CHURCH remains the fertile seedbed where most of what I write grows. The people are gracious and hungry listeners who draw the best out of me—such as it is. The series of messages on Ruth was no exception. Thank you, Bethlehem, for hungering for the word of God through this imperfect servant.

The elders gave me days away over and above my usual writing leave to put the final form of this book together. Brothers, working with you in the leadership of Bethlehem has been for decades a source of relentless joy.

David Mathis, Executive Pastoral Assistant, has become increasingly a source of strength and practical motivation and help not to waste my life—not a day. He keeps my life in order and moves me with great grace from one thing to the other. Without him I would scarcely know what to do next. Thank you, David (and Megan!), for your excellence and friendship.

Noël and Talitha, you are the Ruths in my life. I admire you both, and I love you. Thank you for helping me do what I do.

The son of Ruth, son of David, Son of God is under and over everything. There is no life-giving breath, no final bliss, and no finished book without him. Thank you, Lord Jesus, for shedding your blood so that this sinner can be so blessed.

John Piper
Minneapolis, Minnesota
July 1, 2009

SCRIPTURE INDEX

PERSON INDEX

SUBJECT INDEX

desiringGod

Everyone wants to be happy. Our website was born and built for happiness. We want people everywhere to understand and embrace the truth that *God is most glorified in us when we are most satisfied in him*. We've collected more than thirty years of John Piper's speaking and writing, including translations into more than forty languages. We also provide a daily stream of new written, audio, and video resources to help you find truth, purpose, and satisfaction that never end. And it's all available free of charge, thanks to the generosity of people who've been blessed by the ministry.

If you want more resources for true happiness, or if you want to learn more about our work at Desiring God, we invite you to visit us at desiringGod.org.

desiringGod.org